UNIQUE EATS AND EATERIES

OF

CHICAGO

MATT KIROUAC

Library of Congress Control Number: 2017934681
ISBN: 9781681060903

Printed in the United States of America
17 18 19 20 21 5 4 3 2 1

CONTENTS

ACKNOWLEDGMENTS

First and foremost, I'd like to tip my cap to the great city of Chicago. When I moved here in 2006 from the East Coast, knowing no one and starting from scratch, I wasn't prepared for the overwhelming hospitality and generosity of its residents. From day one, they made me feel at home. It's what kept me in the city all these years and made me fall deeper in love with it year after year. It steered me in the direction my career has taken me, with incredibly gratifying results. So it's an honor to be able to write a book about a part of Chicago I hold dear.

Additionally, there are numerous family members, friends, mentors, and colleagues who have helped shape not only my career, but the person I am today. Without them, this book would have a different author. Therefore, special thanks are due to the following: my always-supportive parents for believing in me and helping me stand on my own two feet, to my husband Bradley for dealing with my stressful moments and always remaining loving and optimistic, to my brother Brian for being a best friend and my favorite person to barhop with, to my sister Emily for cheering me on and being the understanding twin I never knew I needed, to my lovely in-laws, Marianne, Cassie, and Drew, you inspire me to be the best that I can be, and I'm always in awe of your kindness, and to all my friends and colleagues who have been wonderful support systems and motivators over the year. There are far too many to name, but you all know how important you are.

INTRODUCTION

There once was a time, in the not so distant past, that Chicago was primarily regarded as a meat-and-potatoes town, in large part due to its Midwestern locale and reputation as the "hog butcher to the world," with its myriad butchers and meat-processing plants. Oh, how far this mighty city has come in recent decades, though. Nowadays, the Illinois metropolis is home to one of the most exciting, thriving food scenes in the country, with restaurateurs, bakers, chefs, and cooks working together on a cohesive culinary identity that spans mile upon magnificent mile.

Perhaps spurred to defy its prior reputation or its endless comparisons to other cities like New York, Chicago has really raised the bar on its restaurant scene to become a de facto dining destination for travelers near and far. And rightfully so, since the third largest city in the United States boasts unique eats and eateries for all distinguished persuasions. From acclaimed fine dining temples to hole-in-the-wall (sometimes literally) doughnut shops, Chicago has something for everyone. Coupled with its welcoming spirit and its cultural melting pot, this makes for truly one of the most dynamic and multifaceted dining regions anywhere.

Beyond the glitz and glamor of downtown's flashier restaurants, there's much to be discovered throughout Chicago's various neighborhoods. You'll find sensational Mexican food in Pilsen, a Southwest side neighborhood renowned for its Latino heritage and artsy roots. Northwestern enclaves like Lincoln Square are home to everything from Thai takeout counters and German beer halls to whimsical fine dining. Seasoned steakhouses in the Gold Coast do a fine job segueing Chicago's meaty heritage into a new era, while hip hot spots in Wicker Park more than live up to the hype with tacos and cocktails worth the inevitable wait. In the Loop's financial district, bump elbows with politicians at the power lunch capital of the city or meander through glistening food halls lined with everything from barbecue to ramen. Just west of the Loop, Restaurant Row packs a powerhouse punch of heavy-hitting celebrity chefs proving their mettle with some of the most inventive dishes in the country (and some of the most hard-to-snag reservations to match). Or right nearby, queue up in the morning at a time-tested diner for addictive donuts and omelets the size of hubcaps.

That juxtaposition of old and new, haute and frills-free is what makes Chicago's eclectic dining landscape so refreshingly unique. Without any sense of pretense, eateries throughout the city offer a taste of originality and more importantly, palpable passion. Whether it's a taco or a tasting menu, a scoop of gelato or a piping hot crock of moules-frites, it all collectively works together to form a peerless patchwork of culinary experiences.

UNIQUE EATS AND EATERIES

OF

CHICAGO

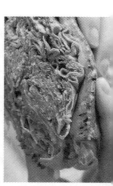

Elaborate tasting menus meet intimate BYOB atmosphere

Who says fine dining and tasting menus automatically entail buttoned-up suit jackets and white tablecloths? Certainly not Jake Bickelhaupt and Alexa Welsh, the husband-wife duo who have seemingly made it their life's mission to thoroughly alter the perception of upscale dining.

Located along a harried, nondescript stretch of Uptown, a neighborhood more renowned for pho than tasting menus, 42 grams initially originated as an in-home supper club called Sous Rising, run by Bickelhaupt (the chef) and Welsh (the hostess). Together, they championed the idea that elaborate, contemporary cookery could be served in multi-course degustations within the confines of a casual, comfortable environment, free of stuffy service, overpriced wine pairings, and white tablecloths. That dream begat 42 grams, a concept that seamlessly bridges the gap between homey supper club and starry-eyed destination dining.

Unlike most fine-dining destinations, 42 grams flies in the face of tradition. Not only is the neighborhood an unassuming locale for such an experience, but the restaurant sports only eighteen seats in a single room that looks like the foyer of a Victorian home—albeit a Victorian home where guests can mosey up to a kitchen counter and dine while gawking at culinary precision. The idea is to curate an experience akin to a private dinner party, but one hosted by much more talented friends than you're probably accustomed to. An alum of places like Schwa and Alinea, Bickelhaupt brings a lot of pedigree to the table here, showcasing his proclivity for seasonally driven new American cuisine in vibrant, stunning, new ways. One multi-course meal might include cultured barley porridge with crispy pork jowl, pig heart, housemade barley koji, and grapefruit; or Skuna Bay salmon brined in barrel-aged lapsang souchong tea with spent malted barley and hops, housemade miso, and chanterelle dashi; or even Wagyu with barrel-fermented soy sauce grilled over binchotan with beef and bone marrow.

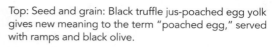

Top: Seed and grain: Black truffle jus-poached egg yolk gives new meaning to the term "poached egg," served with ramps and black olive.

Bottom: Cultured barley: Cultured barley and koji tastes like a hike through the forest, with spruce jus, fermented oxalis roots, allium, and frizzled enoki mushroom.

The restaurant provides BYO wine suggestions on their FAQ page for their current menus. Visit 42 grams's website to view their video tasting menus and gather a sense for what you're getting into.

Of the prized few seats at 42 grams—ten at a communal table and eight at the kitchen counter—reservations must be snagged via tickets off 42 grams's website. Expect to pay upwards of $250 per person for the pleasure, which is indeed worthwhile for such a distinguished experience as this. The restaurant is also unique among its fine-dining compatriots thanks to its BYOB status, which helps ease the sting of the cost. It's yet another way that Bickelhaupt and Welsh manage to freshen up the timeworn tradition of fine dining, which, when coupled with its unexpected locale and intimate ambience, truly lives up to the definition of destination dining.

4662 N Broadway St.
www.42gramschicago.com

312 CHICAGO

Hobnob with politicians and power lunchers at this Italian fixture in the Theatre District

Long before Chicago got hit with a tidal wave of new Italian restaurants, there was 312 Chicago. The Loop restaurant, adjacent to the Kimpton Hotel Allegro Chicago, has been a classic mainstay for locals and visitors alike for years. But beyond any mere Italian restaurant, there's more than meets the eye to 312 Chicago: it's a showcase for Luca Corazzina, an Italian-born chef who brought his penchant for regional Northern Italian fare to the heart of Chicago; it's one of the most prominent pre- or post-show places to go for dinner in the Theatre District; and it's a real power player in regard to hosting the city's political elite—after all, City Hall is directly across the street. On any given day, you may bump elbows with a district attorney over lunch. Or you might sample a pasta recipe handed down from the chef's mother. Or you might do both at the same time. The possibilities really run the gamut.

The chef was reared in Padova, Italy, where he developed a passion for cooking from his chef mother, whom he worked alongside at her restaurant for four years, starting at age sixteen. It was here where he formed his culinary philosophy of using the best ingredients and not over-manipulating them, but rather highlighting them in

"Our clientele for breakfast and lunch consists mostly of politicians, judges, and lawyers," explains Corazzina. "I have cooked for many notable politicians over the years and it's definitely been an honor for me to cook for mayors, congressmen, and our alderman. I think my fondest memory is when Illinois Secretary of State Jesse White dined for lunch and spoke Italian to me."

Top Left: Charcuterie and cheese are 312 Chicago's bread and butter. Photo by Colin Beckett.

Above Left: Serving much more than pasta, Luca Corazzina offers elegant entrees like perfectly seared salmon. Photo by Jason Little.

Above Right: The chef pays homage to his homeland by filling his menu with regional Italian seafood.

wholesome, thoughtful ways. When his family moved to Chicago in 1986, Corazzina began working in his family's restaurant—in Little Italy, naturally. After stints cooking in Florida, he returned to his adopted hometown to open Figo and Prosecco before landing at 312 Chicago. Here, he cooks dishes both rustic and chic, all with a nod toward Northern Italian tradition, like black truffle fried polenta with Taleggio fondue, house-made lasagna enlivened with basil pesto, and roasted pork chops with black Tuscan kale, potato cakes, and brandy cream sauce.

For all its metropolitan surroundings and its political bluster, 312 Chicago still feels like the homey family restaurant in the Italian countryside that Corazzina first fell in love with growing up. It feels like the kind of Italian restaurant that can transport guests and inspire newfound love for a cuisine they thought was all too familiar.

136 N LaSalle St.
312-696-2420
www.312chicago.com

5411 EMPANADAS

A taste of Argentina in Chicago

How does a humble little dumpling take over the Chicago food world? The story of 5411 Empanadas, an American dream-style success story for the ages, went from Argentina to a Chicago apartment before hitting the big time. It's all courtesy of three Argentine expat friends, Nicolas Ibarzabal, Mariano Lanfranconi, and Andrés Arlia, all of whom shared the simple vision of bringing a nostalgic taste of their homeland to their adopted city of Chicago.

Each came to the city for different reasons: Ibarzabal moved here to attend Northwestern University, Lanfranconi was Ibarzabal's best friend from Argentina who came to study at the University of Chicago, and Arlia was working at Leo Burnett after moving to Chicago from Miami. Each had a craving for empanadas, something sorely lacking in Chicago. So the three men started making empanadas out of Ibarzabal's downtown apartment, with the help of their wives and some recipe advice from their grandmothers.

Original flavors—still fan favorites to this day—were beef, chicken, spinach, corn, and ham and cheese, all classic-inspired combos that were eventually joined by novelties like bacon-date-goat cheese and ratatouille. Though none of the empanada entrepreneurs had restaurant or chef experience, they each brought something unique to the table, what with Ibarzabal's managerial skills, Lanfranconi's PhD in economics helping on the numbers side, and Arlia's advertising

The 5411 Empanadas truck, one of the first of its kind to hit the streets in Chicago several years ago, is now a frequent fixture at summer events and street festivals all over town. Follow along on Twitter and keep an eye out for the signature bright blue truck.

Top Left: From a food truck to an empanada empire, 5411 has come a long way in recent years.

Above Left: The meatier options, like Malbec beef, are handheld comfort food.

Above Right: Each location sports a distinct style to match the neighborhood, like this simple and sleek design for Southport Avenue.

expertise lending itself to the company's website design and creative development. After delivering empanadas to friends and parties, they upped their production by renting space in the shared-use commercial space Kitchen Chicago and creating a business out of it, naming it 5411 Empanadas after the international dialing code for Buenos Aires.

This was followed by a food truck, which grew their business and visibility exponentially, eventually paving the way for their ultimate goal of opening a storefront. First came a restaurant in Lakeview, followed by a new location and production facility in Bucktown. It's the second outpost—a central production hub that could support the truck and new storefronts—that allowed the burgeoning restaurateurs to expand at a rapid clip. Soon, locations in the Loop, Wicker Park, and West Lakeview were up and running, and with year-to-year business growing by 50 percent, they were selling more than one million empanadas annually.

Most recently, 5411 Empanadas branched out to new territory with locations in Miami and Houston. From a homesick pipe dream to a Chicago-born empire, 5411 Empanadas is the entrepreneurial dream come true for three friends with a shared passion.

Multiple locations
5411empanadas.com

ACADIA

Maine-inspired fine dining in the South Loop

Everything about Acadia is a surprise. From the offbeat location along a quiet, residential corridor in the South Loop to the chef's serendipitous love affair with Maine, Acadia is truly unlike any other fine-dining institution in Chicago. It's all courtesy of chef/owner Ryan McCaskey, a man with a love for New England and a penchant for the irreverent. His passion for the East Coast is a fortuitous one, as McCaskey was born in Vietnam and adopted just after the Vietnam War ended. Raised in the Chicago suburbs, his family traveled frequently to Deer Isle, Maine, instilling a love for the region for the burgeoning chef. He also clocked time working at the state's acclaimed Goose Cove Lodge after attending culinary school.

To this day, the chef rigorously sources Maine blueberries, insisting that their size, texture, and flavor are superior. Acadia serves as a glorious homage to the Northeast, housed inside an utterly nondescript building in an area populated by residential high-rises. Once inside, guests are whisked away to a pastoral, warm setting, like a chic beachside cottage.

While lobster rolls are available in the front bar area, things are decidedly more upscale in the main dining room, a spacious and Zen-like setting outfitted with large tables, tree branches, and sandy-hued decor. Here, guests choose between tasting menus of varying lengths, each one loaded with one surprise after another, from pig heart tartare to a basket of beef brisket threads designed to resemble

Some of my fondest memories were from childhood summers in Maine. What I find inspiring now is not only the actual gorgeous location, but the product coming from there, the people and relationships I've forged there, and the way of life there." –Ryan McCaskey

8

Above Left: Chef/owner Ryan McCaskey has come a long way in realizing his dream.

Top Right: The main dining room is a beauty.

Bottom Right: Not your average salad course.

a nest, filled with potato and egg—it's like an all-American diner hash on steroids. Of course, McCaskey slips in quirky tributes to New England throughout each tasting, be it a dainty, bite-sized lobster roll amuse-bouche or a medley of clams and cod immersed in chowder sauce. The chef makes an annual pilgrimage to Maine in order to recharge and dig up fresh inspiration and ideas for his ever-evolving menus.

It's a far cry from Deer Isle to the South Loop, but McCaskey's food serves as an apt snapshot of his upbringing, one that's been filled with fortuitous surprises.

1639 S Wabash Ave.
312-360-9500
www.acadiachicago.com

AL'S №1 ITALIAN BEEF

Chicago's most iconic sandwich got its start in Little Italy

In the lexicon of classic Chicago eats, there's deep-dish pizza, there's hot dogs, and there's Italian beef. Although less universally prominent than pizza and hot dogs, Italian beef sandwiches are integral to Chicago's food heritage, and few places can lay claim to such heritage as Al's #1 Italian Beef.

The frills-free sandwich shop in Little Italy dates back to 1938, when Al Ferrari honed his recipe for sandwich success along with his sister and brother-in-law. This was a time when meals were assembled more out of Great Depression necessity than luxury. During a time when meat was expensive and in scant supply, Ferrari attempted to stretch his provisions as far as possible by slicing beef razor thin and piling it on fluffy Italian bread. The result is Chicago's answer to Philadelphia's cheesesteak, sporting similarly tender threads of meat but served au jus with peppers in lieu of provolone. After concocting the deceptively simple formula in his home kitchen, Ferrari and his family took it to the streets, selling sandwiches from a humble sidewalk stand before putting down restaurant roots on Taylor Street.

To this day, diners still flock to this sandwich Mecca to gobble Italian beefs from the standing-room-only eatery, hunched over saucers of warm jus for dipping. Over the decades, they've outfitted the menu with snappy Polish sausages, tamales, and hot dogs, but the heart of Al's remains the sandwich that became a Chicago icon.

Multiple locations, including the original at 1079 W Taylor St.
312-226-4017
www.alsbeef.com

Top: Al's #1 Italian Beef has been a Taylor Street staple for decades.

Bottom Left: If you like it spicy, get giardiniera added to your sandwich for some added punch.

Bottom Center: Here's how it goes down: order sandwich at the counter, scarf said sandwich at counter top, leave happy.

Bottom Right: Whether you order it straight-up meaty or heaped with giardiniera and peppers, Al's Italian beef is a thing of beauty.

ANN SATHER

It's like dining at grandma's house, assuming grandma makes really good Swedish pancakes

Ann Sather is an easy restaurant to find. Simply follow the inviting aroma of freshly baked cinnamon rolls down Belmont Avenue in Lakeview to this longstanding breakfast staple.

This Swedish-accented restaurant, in business since 1945, has a lot more than cinnamon rolls, but the pastries have become as iconic as deep-dish pizza and hot dogs in Chicago. The woman behind it all was born to be a restaurant owner. Although she didn't get into the industry until later in life, Ann Sather was always the type of matriarchal character who wanted to feed and nourish others, the type of person who exuded hospitality and warmth, treating everyone like family.

These are keystones of a family restaurant, and they're the sentiments that have maintained Ann Sather as a legendary Chicago fixture. Opportunity came knocking in 1945, when the owners of Lakeview restaurant retired, leaving a vacant space. Sather quit her longtime job to open her dream diner, which she founded on the wholesome concepts of homemade food, affordable prices, and an inviting family-friendly atmosphere.

For generations, customers have swooned over her omelets, Benedicts, and Swedish pancakes with tangy lingonberry sauce. Sather ran her restaurant for thirty-five years before retiring herself, selling it to Tom Tunney, a talented up-and-comer who has helped the business's continued success in the years since Sather's passing.

He has also maintained the all-important sense of hospitality established by Sather. Perhaps nothing personifies her enduring characteristic quite like the restaurant's now-legendary cinnamon rolls. These impossibly doughy delicacies are served fresh from the oven, doused in warm icing, and filled to the brim with gooey cinnamon and brown sugar.

Although they they might cause you to fill up before the entrees arrive, it's a struggle worth having. From the rolls to the sunny ambience, Sather's legacy is alive and well at one of Chicago's quintessential breakfast spots.

Top: Not everything is sweet at Ann Sather. Try any of the restaurant's incomparable egg dishes, like the crab cake eggs Benedict.

Bottom Left: The perfect combo of sweet and savory, the Monte Cristo plate features eggs, fruit preserves, and ham over French toast.

Bottom Center: Easily Ann Sather's most iconic creation, the cinnamon rolls are an essential snack to start any breakfast.

Bottom Right: One of the most popular orders, the crepe-like Swedish pancakes come with a splash of tangy lingonberry jam.

Multiple locations, including the original at 909 W Belmont Ave.
Original: 773-348-2378
www.annsather.com

ANTIQUE TACO

Contemporary tacos and old-timey antiques

It's not too often that the owners of a taqueria also happen to be ardent antiquers. Just when you thought you'd seen it all when it comes to taquerias, along comes Antique Taco, filling the very precise niche of gourmet taco shop-meets-antique store that's equal to tortillas and kitsch, Chicago never knew it needed.

Dynamic husband and wife team Rick and Ashley Ortiz have combined their dual passions, and the pair managed to create something wholly unique for Chicago's colorful and expansive taco scene.

Located in Wicker Park and sharing a neighborhood with Big Star begs the inevitable comparison between the two taco joints, but rest assured that Antique Taco stands on its own merits. The focus is on the food at this adorable counter-service spot, and rather than serve straightforward street tacos, chef Rick prepares dishes that are more akin to composed entrees that just so happen to be wrapped in tortillas. The kitchen gets crafty with taco combinations such as grilled rib eye with caramelized poblanos and onions and Cheez Whiz and crispy fish tempura with sriracha tartar sauce, smoked cabbage, chives, and sesame. Don't stop at the tacos, though. You won't want to miss the habanero popcorn or duck enchiladas with peanut butter mole and blackberry crema fresca—a savory and elegant riff on a PB&J. Chase your meal with a chocolate and marshmallow filled pop tart and wash it all down with an horchata milkshake or a rosemary-infused margarita.

Now there's more Antique Taco to love, as the couple expanded to Bridgeport with a new location and another one in downtown's Revival Food Hall.

Left: The crispy fish tacos are like fish and chips, but instead of fries it's a tortilla with sriracha, smoked cabbage, and sesame.

Right: The owners pillage Midwestern antique shops to fill up their shelves with unique finds.

The food may be progressive, but the space is full of vintage charm. Designed by Ashley, a meticulous antique hunter with an eye for detail (she frequently roves the Midwest looking for original antiques to stock her shelves), the space is rife with everything from pencils and hats to blankets and Golden Girls paraphernalia. Nostalgic Americana and Mexican street food don't seem like such an obvious pairing at first, but Antique Taco is here to prove it's a match made in heaven.

Wicker Park:
1360 N Milwaukee Ave.
773-687-8697

Bridgeport:
1000 W 35th St.
773-823-9410

www.antiquetaco.com

AU CHEVAL

Chicago's most famous burger and other modern diner comforts

What happens when a burger reaches Beyoncé-level fame? Three-hour wait times at Au Cheval is what happens. Although a modern, dimly lit American diner at heart, with abundant menu items like fried bologna and chicken, the unabashedly decadent burger at this West Loop hot spot has usurped everything else in the kitchen to become the single most buzzed-about dish in Chicago. But when a single menu item amasses such hype, it has a lot to live up to. It's sort of like Mt. Rushmore in a way—when people visit the monument after a lifetime of hype, expectations are extreme.

In short, the Au Cheval burger is the Mt. Rushmore of burgers. Once you've endured the inevitable delay (fortunately, there are about one thousand bars and restaurants in the direct vicinity where you can drink a beer while you wait), the beefy holy grail will not disappoint. Although modest in scope, all the elements are perfectly executed and harmonious, from the impossibly luscious beef patties and gooey American cheese to the thick-cut bacon, runny egg, and buttery bun. The fact that this behemoth is so unapologetic in its excess just makes it that much better—the "single" patty cheeseburger actually comes with two thin patties, and the "double" has three. You have Hogsalt Hospitality to thank for that. The restaurant group is one of the most exciting and dynamic to emerge in Chicago in recent years, in part due to owner Brendan Sodikoff's fearless embrace of indulgence. While at some of his other concepts this means barbecue, deep bowls of ramen, or doughnuts the size of your torso, Au Cheval is all about the Americana. And nothing truly personifies Americana quite like a multi-patty burger.

800 W Randolph St.
312-929-4580
auchevalchicago.com

Top: This isn't your average diner. Photo by Kari Skaflen

Bottom Left: Save room for dessert, because the decadent mille-feuille is not to be missed.

Bottom Right : This is the kind of place where putting an egg on things is highly encouraged.

Looking for a midnight snack that doesn't come from your refrigerator? Au Cheval offers a killer version of chilaquiles after midnight only.

The homey neighborhood cafe every neighborhood craves

For some people, great ideas are found where they'd least expect them. This is certainly true of Baker & Nosh owner Bill Millholland, a gentleman who hadn't considered a career in bakeries before falling into it by fortuitous happenstance.

He initially attended Indiana University to study French and Japanese, a pretty far cry from the croissants and sourdough he's revered for these days. While he always had a fondness for cooking and baking, it wasn't something he considered as a viable career path until his position as product manager for CBS Television was nixed. But when one door closes, another opens, and in Millholland's case, that second door led him to culinary school. He took it as a time to recalibrate his life and pursue something he had always loved.

After graduating from The French Culinary Institute in New York City, he realized his true passion leaned more toward the baking and pastry side of the industry, so he spent time working in bakeries and even clocking time as an instructor at Tuscany's Toscana Saporita Cooking School. Chicago came calling when he accepted a position as a chef instructor at Le Cordon Bleu College of Culinary Arts, something that helped pave the way for opening his own business in 2012 with Baker & Nosh. For Millholland, the cafe represents

"A big part of our business philosophy is our commitment to playing an important role in our community and maintaining great relationships with our customers and neighbors," explains Millholland. "We truly take pride in every aspect of owning a neighborhood business."

Top Left: From biscotti to coffee cake, if you've got a sweet tooth, you've come to the right place.

Above Right: The Uptown bakery gives new meaning to the Midwestern nickname "America's Bread Basket."

Above Left: Fresh-baked bread + crisp greens + tender meat = sandwich perfection.

the culmination of a career—the icing on the cake, if you will—marked by passion and perseverance, one that took him from one job to another, across the globe and back, to a place where he could combine his loves for baking and education.

Along with business partner Terry Groff, Millholland operates Baker & Nosh as the quintessential neighborhood bakery, the kind of homey, welcoming alcove that's mostly a relic in modern-day metropolises. On any given day, Millholland can be found hosting bread classes while customers commune over pastries or stock up on snacks to take home. It's a rare gem in a fast-paced world dominated by food trends and hot spots, and it prides itself on a reliable roster of provisions like potato dill bread, coffee cake, brownies, ham and cheese croissants, and more.

There's also a concise selection of prepared dishes, like soups, sandwiches, frittatas, and stratta studded with seasonal vegetables. It's easy to see why locals are constantly coming back for more.

1303 W Wilson Ave.
773-989-7393
EDGEWATER
5600 N Ridge Ave

www.bakerandnosh.com

BAND OF BOHEMIA

From culinary beers and craft coffee to tasting menus, this place does it all

The first Michelin-starred brewpub was born out of the simple-sounding goal of raising the bar on bar fare. For the all-star team behind Ravenswood's Band of Bohemia, this didn't just mean getting fancy with chicken wings; this meant serving barramundi as part of a tasting menu, infusing pisco cocktails with macerated figs, and brewing beers inspired by breads that one of the co-owners baked while working at Chicago's world-famous Alinea. Every component of this highly ambitious, grandiose brewpub, bar, and restaurant is in harmonious synergy, thanks to the "band members" lending their individual expertise to a larger equation.

The head brewer is Michael Carroll, a chef with experience at places like Bouchon in Napa and Alinea, where he served as the restaurant's only baker. Some of his breads for the restaurant have inspired recipes for beer at Band of Bohemia, like an orange chicory rye that became one of Carroll's first brews. It's also what set the Band apart as a "culinary brewpub," where food and cooking inspire the beers and work in tandem with the kitchen.

Another Alinea alum, Craig Sindelar, is the director of operations and co-owner and, along with Carroll, designed the gloriously sprawling space that boasts a massive open kitchen, soaring chandelier-clad ceilings, and a bar overlooking the microbrewery. He also brings his sommelier chops to the restaurant, having served on wine duty at San Sebastian's Akelarre Restaurant and Alinea.

A more recent feature from Band of Bohemia is bottled beer, sold at select restaurants and retail establishments like Bottles and Cans, Printer's Row Wine Shop, Perman Wine Selections, The Beer Temple, Boeufhaus, and of course, Alinea.

Top Left: seasonal, eclectic cuisine dominates the food menus at Band of Bohemia. Photo by Nick Robins Photography

Above Left: Between house-brewed beers and craft cocktails, the bar program has a knack for a variety of beverages. Photo by Rudy Rubio

Above Right: With soaring ceilings, a wide-open kitchen and chic lounge chairs, this isn't your average brewpub. Photo by Rudy Rubio

Then there's Matt DuBois, the culinary member of the band who presides over the kitchen, serving up elevated bar food and tasting menus to echo the culinary-inspired brews, wines, and crafty cocktails. A Michigan native, he clocked time at local standouts like Crofton on Wells and EL Ideas, plus restaurants in Portland, Oregon, before joining Band of Bohemia to dazzle diners with wholly unique "brewpub" fare like roasted salsify root with preserved Burgundy truffle and a parsnip dessert course with lemon meringue, parsnip cake, and parsnip-apple foam.

In case all that isn't impressive enough, even Band of Bohemia's coffee and tea program boasts an Alinea vet. As do the beer and wine pros, Tom Santelle keeps food and beverage pairings in mind with his coffee and tea offerings, designed to balance acid, sugar, and other components to supplement both the food and the beer. By amassing a veritable dream team of talent and innovation, Band of Bohemia not only rethinks the concept of the brewpub entirely, but breaks new ground in terms of how food, beer, wine, cocktails, and coffee can interact.

4710 N Ravenswood Ave.
773-271-4710
www.bandofbohemia.com

The best heirloom Southern cooking north of the Mason-Dixon Line

It pays to do your homework. This is abundantly clear at Andersonville's venerable Big Jones, a Southern restaurant that goes far beyond your standard fried chicken, biscuits, and tasso ham—although those are all present and accounted for and wildly delicious. With executive chef and owner Paul Fehribach at the helm, Big Jones is a Southern restaurant with big ambitions, and he achieves those ambitions by pouring through more regional history books than most people do in their entire schooling career.

A quick glance at his dining menus, which include brunch, lunch, and dinner, will reveal items that look more like textbook chapter headings than dishes. This includes Reezy-Peezy ca. 1730, farmhouse chicken and dumplings ca. 1920, and Virginia fried steak ca. 1834. Fehribach doesn't just cook, he resurrects real-deal Southern-style cuisine with a serious commitment to historical accuracy, so much so that a mere spoonful of grits feels like a trip through time to another era entirely. An Indiana native

For Fehribach, inspiration comes from three primary sources. "One, I read a lot of old cookbooks. I look for pre-industrial food books so that the recipes aren't tainted by processed foods or products. I want real, honest cooking from raw ingredients. Second, I follow and study the Southern Foodways Alliance closely; they do incredible work documenting and celebrating the diverse food cultures of the changing South, so I always learn something new, and it regularly influences my cooking. Third, I find inspiration and ideas in ingredients. Whether it's a vegetable, animal, or grain, when I'm able to work with beautiful heritage ingredients, I find that tastes and textures can put us in touch with our past, our ancestors."

Left: Typical cornbread has got nothing on Big Jones's Owendaw spoon bread. Photo by Owendaw

Right: The charming dining room has the feel of a Lowcountry home. Photo by Grant Kessler

with his heart in the South and idols like Edna Lewis, the chef puts a lot of effort into researching vintage recipes and traditions, as well as sourcing the best local ingredients and making just about everything in-house. He credits his upbringing amidst Southern Indiana farm culture as helping him personally identify with cooking Southern-style.

Since opening Big Jones in 2008, he has become increasingly entrenched in the culture of the cuisine he loves so much, and the concept has gradually progressed to become more rooted in history. Nowadays, instead of a hodgepodge of typical Southern comfort foods, Big Jones delves into antiquated regional food lore with dishes inspired by New Orleans, the Gulf Coast, Carolina Lowcountry, and Appalachia. Fehribach refers to his style as Southern heirloom cooking, concentrating on sustainably grown heritage and heirloom grains and livestock, with numerous items on the dinner menu highlighting particular historical epochs.

The menu articulates precisely when dishes originated, calling attention to the era from which Big Jones derives its inspiration. Dishes are stitched together from olden Southern cookbooks and extensive research on Fehribach's part, who's on a mission to educate customers on the rich history of America's Southern echelons. While many dishes appear complex, Big Jones is still filled with casual items, from pimiento cheeseburgers and po' boys to shrimp 'n' grits and fried chicken dinners. Components on the menu change frequently, as Fehribach is a major supporter of seasonality. The restaurant makes a lot of its own preserves and pickles, so as to offer summer fruit preserves in the winter and add pops of color and flavor during the times of year when we crave it most.

The restaurant is leisurely and comfortable in a refined sort of way. Just as the food is transportive, the space makes guests feel like they're dining in the South. It has the feel of a Southern parlor-meets-shotgun house, lending a homey and humble atmosphere to the space.

5347 N Clark St.
773-275-5725
bigjoneschicago.com

BIG STAR

The hippest honky-tonk north of the border

In many ways, despite its humble appearance and honky-tonk roots, Big Star is responsible for pushing Chicago into the uppermost echelons of ultimate food cities. Why? Because when Big Star made its splashy debut in Wicker Park, it marked a turning point where food of the highest quality suddenly became accessible to all. With a famous chef like Paul Kahan manning the menu and bracingly fresh ingredients outfitting the kitchen, Big Star suddenly brought fine dining-caliber cuisine to a whole new level that can be enjoyed by all—assuming, of course, that you're willing to endure the hour-long wait times to snag a seat on the coveted patio. For One Off Hospitality Group, the company behind Big Star, the casual taqueria and bar marked an opportunity to prove that innovation and inspiration are not confined to the higher end. After road-tripping through Southern California for inspiration, Kahan and company sought to bring something wholly unique to Chicago by combining top-tier tacos with an ambience that feels entrenched in the community (indeed it is, considering Big Star is housed in a mid-century gas station). And so they did, opening a bar and restaurant that does justice to a city renowned for its taco culture, with the largest population of Mexican expats outside of California. Tortillas are made fresh by hand throughout the day and long into the night, folded around succulent pineapple-glazed pork or smoky charred nopales. Whiskey and

Breakfast tacos are a recent addition to Big Star's repertoire, and while the bar doesn't open until 11:00 a.m. for lunch, customers can get their a.m. fix from the adjoining takeout window on weekends.

Top Left: The pineapple-splashed al pastor pork tacos are a rightful crowd favorite. Photo by Edouard Pierre

Above Right: During the warmer months, the Big Star patio is the place to dine and drink al fresco. Photo by Cassie Stadnicki

Above Left: Come for the tacos, stay because you've had a lot of tequila. Photo by Lucy Angel

tequila dominate the cocktail menu, a collection of new and vintage cocktails, plus margarita pitchers that make Big Star such a hit with groups. The whole experience simultaneously captures the essence of a frills-free California honky-tonk while maintaining a serious commitment to the utmost quality. It's the kind of passion that helped pave the way for a new era of casual restaurants and bars in Chicago, and in many ways, across the country.

1531 N Damen Ave.
773-235-4039
www.bigstarchicago.com

BIRRIERIA ZARAGOZA

A family-run Mexican eatery with a knack for goat

Some of the best restaurants are born out of homesickness. Such is the case with Birrieria Zaragoza, a pint-sized family-run restaurant in Chicago's Archer Heights neighborhood on the Southwest side. Opened in 2007 by Juan Zaragoza, a former *Chicago Tribune* employee with no prior restaurant experience, the restaurant simply stemmed from a nostalgic yearning for the food of his native Jalisco, Mexico. And so he spent years studying, cooking, and traveling back and forth between Mexico and the United States in order to bring a taste of his childhood to his adopted hometown of Chicago. Juan and the rest of the Zaragozas take serious pride in their namesake restaurant, which emphasizes goat dishes largely unseen in Chicago.

Everything is made from scratch at this humble operation, with a small menu revolving around birria, a specialty of Zaragoza's hometown of La Barca. Goats are butchered in-house, steamed for hours, marinated in mole, and roasted, infusing flavor and tenderness throughout the meat. Bowls of warming consommé, strewn with succulent morsels of goat, radiate heady aromas and flavors unlike anything else in the city. It's all augmented by a cornucopia of customizable supplements, like raw onions, fresh cilantro, lime, chilies, and housemade hot sauce.

Feel free to fill it up, because each addition lends a welcome layer of texture and flavor to this fine bowl of soul-soothing nourishment. Warm housemade corn tortillas are at their best when dredged through the goat stew. Birrieria Zaragoza may be tiny and

Order your birria "surtido" to try a sampling of goat parts. And be sure and visit on the weekend to try their machito, aka offal soup.

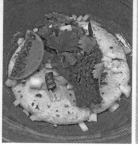

Left: Succulent meats, slowly cooked for hours until fork-tender and fragrant, are the name of the game at this Archer Heights gem.

Center: Tacos don't come any fresher (or get any more authentic) than the ones at Birrieria Zaragoza.

Right: Goat birria is a signature favorite, featuring tender goat meat and rich consommé, adorned with customizable add-ons like onions, cilantro, lime, and chilies.

unassuming, but the kitchen breeds talent. Son Jonathan Zaragoza has already made a name for himself in the Chicago culinary world, serving as executive chef at Masa Azul before the age of twenty-five, drawing lines of customers for hot chicken at The Budlong, and more. Without question, he's one of the most promising talents in the Chicago dining scene.

His family's restaurant is not a fancy place by any means; it's pretty basic and taqueria-like, but the atmosphere is friendly and welcoming. The sense of family and warmth is palpable, which makes the whole experience that much more enjoyable. When someone follows his heart and chases his dreams, it really makes the overall experience a heartwarming one.

4854 S Pulaski Rd.

773-523-3700

www.birrieriazaragoza.com

BISTRO CAMPAGNE

A romantic taste of France in the heart of Lincoln Square

Romance and farm-to-table don't often go hand in hand, but Bistro Campagne is the rare exception that mixes the two to great effect. One of the most revered restaurants in Lincoln Square, Bistro Campagne has been a pillar in Chicago's farm-to-table movement, thanks to late Chef Michael Altenberg. Grounded in French bistro fare and schooled in classic technique, Altenberg worked tirelessly with farmers to curate a menu of locally sourced French classics, and, thanks to Chef Luke Creagan, the restaurant is still going strong and adhering to that vision after his unexpected death in 2012.

Today, Creagan continues Altenberg's legacy of fusing Midwestern ingredients with French tradition. As it turns out, this legacy makes for quite a romantic pairing too. If a restaurant were to capture the heartwarming essence of *Lady and the Tramp*, that restaurant would be Bistro Campagne. Though in this case, the spaghetti would be replaced by coq au vin.

The space feels like a genuine slice of France in Chicago, both in ambience and flavor. Appetizers such as tartare, charcuterie, and bubbling hot onion soup—all made with locally sourced meats

"I am so privileged to work for such an already well established restaurant that has tremendous support, especially from our Lincoln Square neighborhood," says Creagan. "We also strive to keep with the times and trends as so many other restaurants are doing in this amazing melting pot city of culinary goodies."

Top Left: The pastoral patio is a quaint haven for enjoying a romantic dinner and sharing plates of steak frites.

Above Left: Bistro Campagne confit de canard, duck confit is a crowd-pleaser, crispy and golden with cannellini beans, duck fat fingerling potatoes, and saffron aioli. Photo by Anthony Robert La Penna

Above Right: A Lincoln Square fixture for years, Bistro Campagne is a beloved French gem. Photo by Anthony Robert La Penna

and produce, no less—are as authentic as they come, and the same can be said about entrees like roasted chicken, steak frites, and boeuf Bourguignon. The space is as charming as the food; divided into several intimate rooms, it creates the sensation of dining in someone's manor and stealing kisses when the host isn't looking. Like the best Parisian restaurants, Bistro Campagne is romantic to the core, cozy on the inside and warm and lustrous in the outside garden.

4518 N Lincoln Ave.
773-271-6100
www.bistrocampagne.com

BLACKBIRD

The O.G. of Restaurant Row is as good as ever

Over the course of the past decade, Chicago's reputation as a world-class dining city has steadily been on the rise, thanks in large part to pioneering chefs like Paul Kahan. Well before the city was dotted with restaurant group empires like Hogsalt, Heisler Hospitality, Land & Sea Dept., and so many others, there was One Off Hospitality Group and its very first restaurant: Blackbird. At the nexus of that restaurant was executive chef and partner Paul Kahan, a man whose rising star would almost defy his inherent modesty. It's almost surprising to learn that Kahan, who helms some of the city's most influential restaurants and bars, from Big Star to The Violet Hour, comes from such humble origins. The native Chicagoan first got his taste for the food industry helping at his dad's delicatessen, and although he initially embarked on a career in computer science, he fells head over heels (or rather, head over chef clogs) for cooking while working at a restaurant called Metropolis under Erwin Drechsler. Over the course of his fifteen-year tenure working with Drechsler, Kahan formed relationships with local farmers, setting the foundation for a future career rooted in seasonality and locality. He went on to work at Topolobampo under the inimitable Rick Bayless before opening Blackbird in 1999, in a part of town that was then devoid of dining options. The restaurant would quickly rack up the accolades for its forward-thinking contemporary cooking, a style that has evolved over time to stay constantly fresh and innovative. With a menu that changes frequently, each visit brings something new. One night patrons might find sweetbread pastrami and flounder Florentine, while another could offer suckling pig

If you want the Blackbird experience but can't muster the prices, come for lunch. This is a more casual, less expensive alternative to dinner.

Above Left: Diners still flock from near and far for a taste of Paul Kahan's original restaurant. Photo by Doug Fogelson

Top Right: Blackbird, where dessert looks like it belongs in an art gallery. Photo by Sandy Noto

Above Right: Since 1999, Blackbird has been one of Chicago's most essential dining institutions. Photo by Doug Fogelson

pavé and jasmine-scented fluke crudo. The restaurant itself, which Kahan operates alongside A-list business partners Donnie Madia, Eduard Seitan, Terry Alexander, Peter Garfield, and Rick Diarmit, is beautifully minimal and sleek. Almost entirely white, the interior sets an apt blank canvas that allows the gorgeous dishes to shine even brighter. Through it all, Kahan prides himself most on mentoring younger chefs, both through his charitable work with programs like Pilot Light, which empowers school children to make better food decisions through hands-on lessons, and through his employment of up-and-coming chefs, cooks, and pastry chefs. Many successful chefs owe a debt of gratitude to Blackbird and to Kahan, who helped hone their visions and skills within the restaurant's venerable walls.

619 W Randolph St.
312-715-0708
www.blackbirdrestaurant.com

BOKA

Contemporary American cuisine is as stunning as its Lincoln Park space

One of Chicago's most successful restaurant empires began over a cup of coffee between two new friends. Those friends were Kevin Boehm and Rob Katz, a newly introduced duo who were looking to start a new career chapter. While the former had opened and sold restaurants in Florida and Nashville and the latter had gone from options exchange trader to bar operator, both were ready for the next big step of opening a restaurant in Chicago.

Now one of the biggest and most respected restaurant groups in Chicago, Boka Restaurant Group first got its start with its namesake Lincoln Park restaurant in 2003. An instant hit, Boka is the stunning contemporary American restaurant that launched a tidal wave of success that's helped shape Chicago's dining landscape.

While the group has gone on to open some of the most sensational juggernaut restaurants in town (Girl & the Goat, Duck Duck Goat, Momotaro, Swift & Sons), their original remains one of the most timeless destinations in Chicago. That's all thanks to their pioneering efforts set in place at Boka. It helped establish an aesthetic and a company philosophy for the restaurant group to follow, not to mention a penchant for fostering top-tier culinary talent. It's a template they've adapted with aplomb, setting the bar for how restaurants succeed in Chicago and beyond.

"I really enjoy working with all the chefs in the group," says Wolen. "But even more, I enjoy the freedom Kevin and Rob provide us while still giving great direction on how to successfully and sustainably run a business."

Top: Boka has aged quite nicely. Photo by Eric Kleinberg

Bottom Left: Flatbreads at Boka will ruin you for all other pizzas. Photo by Galdones Photography

Bottom Right: The restaurant remains an innovator of contemporary cuisine, serving seasonal and often local ingredients in vibrant new ways. Photo by Galdones Photography

This is where Giuseppe Tentori, one of the city's most charismatic chef talents, rose to serious acclaim before going on to open beloved GT Fish & Oyster and GT Prime with Boka. This is also where chef Lee Wolen advanced his career to the upper echelons by putting his own distinct stamp on seasonal American cuisine, racking up Michelin stars and accolades along the way. For Wolen, helping the metamorphosis of the "old Boka" into the "new Boka" was an exciting challenge, breathing fresh life into the food, the space, and the culture of an established and venerable restaurant like this one. All these years later, Boka is still steadily evolving, constantly adapting to change, and keeping things impressively fresh with ever-changing creations like roasted carrots with vadouvan and smoked feta, shellfish and apple chowder with kombu, and smoked mussels and whole-roasted dry-aged duck with foie gras sausage. From starry-eyed visionaries to lauded empire-builders, Boehm and Katz have come a long way in the industry, and it's all thanks to their inspired partnership that helped launch one of Chicago's most timeless destinations.

Rob and I used to sit across the bar every night at the end of shift in the early days and sketch out the desired path of our company. This was done mostly on cocktail napkins, and many nights we sat there and dreamed of the future over a bottle of wine. The lessons we learned at Boka could fill an entire book, but perhaps our favorite lesson was that the best talent is often homegrown. Ian Goldberg, our VP and partner, started as an opening bartender with basically no experience. In those days, we were not the first look for the people with deep resumes, so we hired a lot of people based solely on character. This is a now a tenet of all that we do." –Kevin Boehm

More than ten years in, the restaurant is better than ever. Photo by Eric Kleinberg

1729 N Halsted St.
312-337-6070
www.bokachicago.com

BOLEO AND VOL. 39

Travel to Peru and a Victorian-style parlor under the same roof

The past couple years have seen a renaissance in the Loop's dining and drinking scene, notably at historic buildings that have been beautifully restored to new glory. The trend started with the Chicago Athletic Association hotel, it continued with The National building and its Revival Food Hall, and it reached an elegant apex with the Kimpton Gray Hotel, housed inside the New York Life Insurance Building, constructed in 1894.

Now, the Financial District building is home to a glamorous hotel that just so happens to contain the ultimate lobby bar and a rooftop restaurant like no other, each one impressively transportive and unique. The former is Vol. 39, a 1940s-inspired bar filled with library-style bookshelves, martinis, caviar, Cognac, and tufted leather couches. The whole thing looks like a room from the board game Clue, but with top-tier hospitality instead of murder.

For Lambert, Boleo's South American roots are near and dear to her heart. Her grandmother is Peruvian, so the restaurant taps into some of the culture she grew up with. In preparing to open the restaurant, she traveled extensively through Peru for research. One of her biggest discoveries was the sheer variety of citrus fruits and their varying acidities, pH levels, and sugars. She even went so far as to create custom citrus blends for Boleo, measuring precise pH levels and mixing different citrus juices to nail different flavor profiles and acid levels for cocktails.

Top Left: This is a no-smoking bar. Except for the smoking cocktails, of course. Photo by David Szymanski

Center Left: Pomp and circumstance is alive and well at Vol. 39, where caviar service is delivered tableside on carts. Photo by David Szymanski

Bottom Left: Why have one martini, when you can order six minis as part of a flight? Photo by David Szymanski

Above Right: From the vintage-inspired couches to the walls of bookshelves, Vol. 39 feels like a bar out of the board game Clue. Photo by Laure Joliet

Fifteen stories up is Boleo, a colorful Peruvian restaurant with Latin-inspired DJ sets, an open-air dining room with a retractable glass roof, and some of the most vibrant cocktails and food in town. Such dynamic and distinctive dining spaces require a deft team to pull it together successfully, and pull it off they do, thanks to chef de cuisine Alexis Hernandez and head bartender Jess Lambert.

Initially inspired to become a chef by his mother, whom he calls a great cook, Peruvian-born Hernandez has pieced together influences from the chefs he's worked with over the years. But it was always those flavorful memories of his mother cooking over firewood in their backyard that filled him with passion and drove him to attend Le Cordon Bleu Peru. Nowadays, his experiences and trajectory culminate with bracing ceviches, South American skewers called anticuchos, and empanadas filled with beef and hard-boiled eggs.

Then there's Lambert, who echoes Hernandez's cooking perfectly by creating drinks that are just as thrilling as the food. At both Vol. 39 and Boleo, she designs cocktails to take guests to another world, be it the Mad Men-era of Americana with Cognac old-fashioneds or the Amazon via drinks splashed with exotic citrons like camu camu and lucuma. Creating two totally different menus for two totally different concepts is a challenge, but she refers to it as the most rewarding thing she's done in her career, exercising her creativity to the max.

It's fitting that restaurants inside a historic landmark building would serve as time machines and airports simultaneously, whisking visitors to a bygone era and an exotic vacation at the same time.

Boleo:
122 W Monroe St.
312-750-9007
www.boleochicago.com

Vol. 39:
39 S LaSalle St.
312-750-9012
www.vol39.com

Top: Boleo's tree-lined bar is sure to transport you to the tropics of South America. Photo by David Szymanski

Bottom Left: Camarones con quinoa is an essential platito, wherein shrimp are coated with crunchy quinoa and served with sweet potato croquettes and passion fruit reduction. Photo by David Szymanski

Bottom Center: Cocktails at Boleo are as lush and vibrant as its tropical motif. Photo by Colin Beckett

Bottom Right: You haven't tasted ceviche like this before. Tart, bracing options at Boleo include the classico, made with whitefish, leche de tigre, and cancha. Photo by David Szymanski

CALUMET FISHERIES

Frills-free shack with a penchant for smoked fish

Calumet Fisheries is a fish shack steeped in serious history. Established in 1928 and purchased in 1948 by brothers-in-law Sid Kotlick and Len Toll, the restaurant is still run by the Kotlick–Toll family. This place evokes a trip back in time, unfettered by trends or other modern elements.

Back in its early days, the smoked fish business was booming, especially in the far South Side area of South Deering, where boats would ride by throughout the day and a largely Scandinavian population would frequent the fishery. Though the times and demographics have changed, not much else has at Calumet Fisheries. Sure, there are a few newer wall ornaments (a picture from Anthony Bourdain's visit, a newspaper article from when The Blues Brothers filmed a bridge jump in front of the shack, a James Beard America's Classics award) and a new ATM, but the heart and soul of the timeworn operation remains intact. To dine here is to open a time capsule—a time capsule perfumed with smoke.

The reason Calumet Fisheries has remained so endearing for so long is simple: the smoked fish is front and center, and they've got decades of experience under their belts to perfect techniques. What makes their fish so special is their process, which begins with drying the skin, then baking the fish before hanging it in their small smokehouse for six hours over a bed of slow-burning wood. It's one of a very few places in Chicago permitted to use wood smoking, largely because that pesky Great Chicago Fire sort of gave wood a bad reputation around here. The attentive, timely process ensures a superior product.

The most popular item is their salmon, which is offered in two varieties—plain (for the smoked fish purists) and pepper and garlic. The menu is vast, sporting smoked trout, sturgeon, sable, and more. Other popular picks are the smoked shrimp and fried shrimp. In addition to the smoky and fried offerings, you can round out your lunch with some of their stellar sides and salads. And by salads, we mean macaroni salad and coleslaw, so don't come here expecting to adhere to a diet. The space is as refreshingly frills-free as the menu

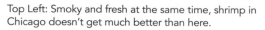

Top Left: Smoky and fresh at the same time, shrimp in Chicago doesn't get much better than here.

Center Left: Pick a nice day to visit, drive your car, scarf your smoked fish on the hood, and watch the boats glide by on the river.

Bottom Left: In the Midwest, where smoked fish is a tragic rarity, Calumet Fisheries reigns supreme.

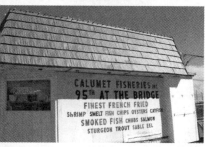

One of the most iconic Chicago-based movie scenes of all time was filmed right in front of Calumet Fisheries. The 95th Street Bridge over the Calumet River is where The Blues Brothers jumped their Bluesmobile.

offerings, with sparse seating options limited to picnic tables outside. Or the hood of your car. The bridge nearby, overlooking the Calumet River, is a nice backdrop, especially when boats chug by. On a nice day, the setting is tranquil and unlike anything else in Chicago, like the true bygone throwback this place is.

3259 E. 95th St.
773-933-9855
www.calumetfisheries.com

CEMITAS PUEBLA

Take your taste buds to Puebla with these massive Mexican sandwiches

While Mexican cuisine is omnipresent throughout Chicago, one regional style oft unseen is that of Puebla. And that's precisely the order of the day at Cemitas Puebla, a unique asset among Chicago's varied Mexican dining landscape. Owner Tony Anteliz still has plenty of family in Puebla, a state in southeastern Mexico categorized by its bold, bracing flavors like adobo chipotle peppers, hearty rolls, hand-pulled cheese, papalo greens, and an abundance of avocado. It's an area that directly inspired him to open Cemitas Puebla, which draws on fond memories of scarfing tacos while visiting his grandma in Mexico.

The restaurant originally operated as a bare-bones storefront in Humboldt Park before moving to the red-hot Fulton Market dining district. Anteliz has since added another outpost in Hyde Park. More than just gaining inspiration from the region, Anteliz goes the extra mile when it comes to sourcing his ingredients, to ensure the utmost authenticity. Actually, make that an extra 2,000 miles. Every several weeks, he makes the trip to Mexico to pick up provisions himself, including regional chilies and stringy Oaxacan cheese.

Naturally, the restaurant's specialty is the cemita, a sandwich unique to the Puebla that packs a hefty punch. Its anatomy includes a dense sesame seed roll layered with mashed avocado, meat, smoky chipotle pepper sauce, and a healthy sprinkling of that shredded Oaxacan cheese. Sandwiches are made to order, and fresh ingredients are layered carefully and thoughtfully.

The restaurant also provides each table with homemade salsas infused with many of the chilies plucked from street markets in Puebla. Of all the cemitas, the Atomica is a crowd favorite, probably because it contains a combination of meats from three of their other sandwiches: the Milanesa, Carne Enchilada, and Jamon.

The rest of the menu is fairly small, with a few chalupas, tacos, and

Above Left: Let the artsy skull be your guide and lead you to your next favorite sandwich.

Top Right: The hulking cemitas sandwiches are no joke. Notably larger than your typical torta and loaded with meat and cheese, they're great to share with a hungry friend.

Bottom Right: They may not be the namesake sandwich, but tacos at Cemitas Puebla are among the best in Chicago.

tortas. Be sure and save room for the Taco Arabe, a hefty burrito-like taco stuffed with juicy spit-roasted pork in a thick, pita-like tortilla.

817 W Fulton Market
312-455-9200
www.cemitaspuebla.com

CHERRY CIRCLE ROOM

A bygone-era Chicago classic gets glamorous new life inside the Chicago Athletic Association

The year was 1890. Olympic athletes and legendary Chicagoans like William Wrigley and Marshall Field were fixtures at the Cherry Circle Room, the restaurant tucked away inside the elite Chicago Athletic Association members' club. They'd clink martini glasses, slurp oysters, and heap caviar on toast.

Today, the tradition lives on, but in a much different form. When the Cherry Circle Room and Chicago Athletic Association re-emerged in their new iterations in 2016, after lying dormant for decades on Michigan Avenue in downtown Chicago, these relics of the city's gilded age found themselves in a fresh spotlight. Nowadays, the Chicago Athletic Association is a luxury boutique hotel, home to some of the hippest and most beautiful dining and drinking spaces in the city.

The cherry atop the metaphorical sundae is Cherry Circle Room, a restaurant that looks plucked out of the *Titanic* era of opulence and glamor, with food and cocktails inspired by the original menus from the late 1800s. So, in a way, you can eat the same kind of food that Olympic gold medal swimmer Johnny Weissmuller once ate.

Cherry Circle Room is joined on the second floor of the Chicago Athletic Association by other spaces from Land and Sea Dept. project development studio. Game Room is a playful nod to the hotel's former life as an athletic members' hub, outfitted with classic equipment like bocce, billiards, chess, and shuffleboard. Then there's Milk Room, a matchbox-sized micro bar from McGee featuring rare spirits and highly elevated takes on cocktails.

Top Left: How about a massive rib eye built for two? This is the Midwest, after all. Photo by Clayton Hauck

Left Center: Whether historically inspired or newfangled, cocktails at Cherry Circle Room come in all kinds of colorful shapes and sizes. Photo by Clayton Hauck

Bottom Left: You know you're in the right place when this light beckons you in for dinner. Photo by Clayton Hauck

Above Right: Make your way to the second floor of the Chicago Athletic Association hotel and step into one of the most beautiful dining rooms and bars in town. Photo by Clayton Hauck

Located in the rear of the second floor (look for the neon cherry sign), this new adaptation is courtesy of Land and Sea Dept., the award-winning outfit behind the likes of Longman & Eagle, Parson's Chicken & Fish, and Lost Lake. With a keen eye for design and a knack for paying homage to the past, the group gussied up the dining room and transformed it into a softly lit, romantic den of wood panels, curved walls, delicate lamps, snug booths, and tableside cocktail service. From poached langoustines and French onion soup to foie gras pâté and skate wing, the dining menus read like a ritzy blast from the past, as do many of the historically inspired cocktails by acclaimed mixology maven Paul McGee—think Pink Squirrels and Whiz-Bangs made with absinthe, pomegranate, and vermouth.

Altogether, Cherry Circle Room is a smart, tasteful homage to Chicago's storied past, and be it 1890 or 2017, it's equally as essential.

12 S Michigan Ave.
312-792-3515
www.lsdatcaa.com/cherry-circle-room

COALFIRE

Thin-crust pizza with an East Coast accent

Coalfire pizza is a genuine slice of originality in Chicago. While so many pizzerias conform to a distinct regional style, be it New York, Chicago deep-dish, or even New Haven, Coalfire colors outside the lines. Opened by Chicagoan Dave Bonomi and Massachusetts native Bill Carroll in 2007, the duo saw a need for something in Chicago that wasn't deep-dish. Especially with so many East Coast expats moving to the Midwest, the demand for thin crust was on the rise, so they decided to answer the call. The result is a casual pizzeria that simultaneously feels like an homage to Boston's Italian North End and the dining culture of Chicago.

Opening an offbeat pizzeria in the land of deep-dish was a bold move for the pizza slingers, but Coalfire has been smokin' hot since opening in West Town in 2007. The name references its unique coal-fired brick oven, the first of its kind in Chicago. Similar to those baked in wood-fired ovens, coal-fired pizzas cook at volcanic temperatures of 800 degrees for about two minutes.

Ovens here run on a combination of clean-burning coal and wood, ensuring that these thin-crust beauties develop a blackened char on the bottom and a blistery edge. Just as charring a marshmallow over a campfire makes for gooey perfection, blistering a thin-crust pizza takes the pie to an ethereal level. Don't be startled by the blackened sections on the crust. It may look burnt, but it's all part of the flavor-building process.

Naturally, fresh dough demands fresh toppings, and Coalfire steps it up by sourcing some of their meats from local butcher shops like Publican Quality Meats and The Butcher & Larder. Cheeses, sauces, and herbs are all fresh and vibrant, and other pizza accents like honey come from Redwing Farms in suburban Harvard, Illinois. The pizzeria adopts the less-is-more approach to toppings, mainly because their thin crust can't support a boatload of accoutrements. They recommend two to three toppings if you're going to customize.

The menu consists mostly of red and white pizzas, aside from a few salads and calzones. The atmosphere at Coalfire is charmingly rustic in a minimalist sense. It's sparse, but the casual and friendly

Top Left: One of the only coal-fired ovens in Chicago can be found inside this West Town pizzeria, churning out some of the best pies in town.

Top Right: Capable of reaching near-volcanic levels of heat, ovens at Coalfire cook pizzas in mere seconds.

Bottom Left: Word of caution: Coalfire may ruin all other pizza for you.

Bottom Right: Pepperoni pizzas get creamy dollops of tangy ricotta.

staff manages to make the unassuming space feel totally warm and inviting. When the owners set out to open Coalfire, they aspired to give Chicago something original that would make its own mark on the city. A decade later and still hotter than ever, it's safe to say they accomplished that goal.

West Town:
1321 W Grand Ave.
312-226-2625

Lakeview:
3707 N Southport Ave.
773-477-2625

coalfirechicago.com

DOUGHNUT VAULT

It's worth the wait at this pint-sized counter for Chicago's best doughnuts

When instant restaurateur and Hogsalt Hospitality founder Brendan Sodikoff converted a small portion of his River North restaurant, Gilt Bar, into a doughnut shop, he changed the paradigm for dining and food trends in Chicago forever. And the lines quickly ensued, routinely winding down the block for a taste of some of the best fried dough in the country. Doughnut Vault not only ignited the doughnut craze in town (something that doesn't appear to ever be subsiding), but it also helped christen a whip-smart new business model for restaurateurs seeking to maximize profit, simply by carving out a portion of an existing business for something fresh and new.

By coupling this model with the inherently low food cost to make doughnuts, even with high-quality ingredients like top-tier butter and chocolate, Doughnut Vault set a new bar for how businesses

Part of the genius and instant success of Doughnut Vault stemmed from Sodikoff's inventive social media work leading up to the opening. Draped in mystery and intrigue, the marketing campaign had Chicagoans eagerly awaiting their first dedicated doughnut shop by perusing the company's vague Tumblr blog, which followed a mystery baker named Francois through various stages of doughnut making. Through gorgeous, drool-worthy photography and social media tease, Sodikoff and company were basically able to solidify Doughnut Vault's credibility well before actually opening.

Top Left: Habit-forming cake doughnuts come in flavors like coconut cream, bursting with rich tropical flavor.

Above Left: No matter which flavor you choose, you're in for a sweet treat.

Above Right: Doughnut Vault exterior current: Customers line up down the block to sink their teeth into some of the very best doughnuts in Chicago.

can rake in the dough from . . . dough. The space is tiny, borderline claustrophobic, with no seats to speak of, but the lines (and the glazed doughnuts) are consistently huge.

The menu features only a handful of flavors, plus rotating daily specials, but these fried beauties speak for themselves, revelatory in their indulgent simplicity. Since the Vault makes only a limited number each day, it's worth getting there on the early side to ensure you get the flavors you want. Old-fashioned buttermilk and gingerbread doughnuts are properly dense and cakey, albeit light and crumbly at the same time.

Meanwhile, impossibly fluffy yeast-raised doughnuts come in much larger glazed varieties, like chocolate and vanilla. The only other option on the menu is coffee. There's a newer location in the West Loop and a mobile operation, The Vault Van, which is easily the prettiest food truck in Chicago.

401 N Franklin St.
doughnutvault.com

Fine dining gets whimsical in Lincoln Square

Dining at Elizabeth is less like a tasting menu experience and more like an idyllic stroll through the woods for your taste buds. That's because calling Iliana Regan a chef is an understatement. The self-taught culinarian is also an avid forager, pillaging forests and fields in the Midwest and combining her findings with elegant whimsy, a combo that sounds like an oxymoron but presents itself on the plate in truly incredible ways.

Reared on a small Midwestern farm, her upbringing inspires Regan, whose underlying ethos is to highlight the purity of local ingredients, in each and every thing she does. Her ever-changing tasting menus at the blink-and-you'll-miss-it Lincoln Square restaurant, which she named after her sister, often sport quirky themes like Downton Abbey, ugly fruit, and Game of Thrones, but they all boast the same central tenet of seasonality and locality.

From foie gras molded into the shape of an adorable owl to popovers with rose petal ice cream and an Earl Grey-cured egg yolk, everything Regan touches is as visually striking as it is uniquely flavorful. Even in terms of ambience, the chef transports guests to her bucolic roots with a folksy and comfortable space reminiscent of a cottage.

4835 N Western Ave.
773-681-0651
www.elizabeth-restaurant.com

Regan expanded her repertoire in 2017 with the opening of Kitsune, an inventive Japanese restaurant located down the street in North Center.

Top Left: You never know what surprises Regan has up her chef sleeves. Like this bear Rice Krispies treat, for instance.

Above Left: This is the rare restaurant that manages to make foie gras adorable—by molding it into the shapes of cute animals.

Above Right: Assuming you don't get lost trying to find it, the restaurant sports a dining room reminiscent of a pastoral cottage.

EVEREST

Elegant French flavors that soar high above the city

For more than thirty years, Everest has soared as a transcendent fine-dining destination in Chicago. Located on the 40th floor of the Chicago Stock Exchange in downtown's Financial District, the restaurant offers a fittingly glorious setting in which to experience chef Jean Joho's illustrious French fare. And considering the panoramic city views, it's really saying something that guests here have a hard time prying their eyes off the beautiful plates that come out of the kitchen as elements of elaborate tasting menus. Each dish is a work of art, a sentiment echoed by the bronze sculptures that bedeck each table and the elegant artwork sourced from the chef's friends.

For Joho, the food and the awe-inspiring ambience are apt odes to his homeland of Alsace, France, a region he champions as having the greatest synergy of wine and food in the country. With a wine portfolio that boasts 1,600 bottles, 350 of which come from Alsace, you'll likely agree. Alsace is where Joho first got a taste of the restaurant world while visiting his aunt's professional kitchen, and later where he apprenticed at world-famous L'Auberge de L'Ill at the ripe age of 13. He knew at a young age that cooking was his calling, a passion that took him to kitchens throughout France, Switzerland, and Italy as part of his burgeoning career. In 1986, Joho opened the restaurant that would become a catapult to international acclaim.

The astonishing thing about Everest is its durability and the timelessness of its cuisine. Unlike seemingly all the other restaurants

Everest is also revered as one of the best fine-dining restaurants for vegetarians. Joho features a designated vegetarian tasting menu, which features ever-changing seasonal dishes like artichoke fricassée, polenta galettes, and Bartlett pear gelée with artisan yogurt glacé.

Top Left: Roasted sea bass with crispy potato and thyme is a throwback to Everest's earliest menus.

Top Right: Between the bronze statues on every table and the panoramic views from the 40th floor of the Chicago Stock Exchange, there's lots to marvel at. Photo by Richard Hellyer

Bottom Left: Though dainty, mignardises and petit fours at Everest are big on flavor, and they end dinner on a very high note. Photo by Richard Hellyer

Bottom Left Center: It doesn't get more classic French than a plate of foie gras. Photo by Richard Hellyer

Bottom Right Center: It may be a French restaurant, but Everest proudly sources and celebrates cheeses from the Midwest. Photo by Richard Hellyer

Bottom Right: Chef Jean Joho has been soaring high atop Chicago's dining scene since 1986. Photo by Anjali Pinto

in town, which live and die by the notion of hot and new, Joho's maintained a restaurant built on enduring tradition and beautiful dishes composed with surgical precision. The lavish service, demure ambience, and pristine cuisine are virtually the same today as they were on opening day, and it's a testament to Joho's vision and skill that Everest still holds an indelible place among the uppermost echelon of Chicago's restaurant elite. There will always be a place for the iconic French restaurant where degustations entail marbré of duck with truffle vinaigrette, oysters with cucumber-Riesling fleurette, scallops with fennel choucroute, and filet of sole meunière with pomme mousseline.

440 S LaSalle St.
312-663-8920
www.everestrestaurant.com

Macanese cuisine makes for a fine taste adventure

Fat Rice is one of the most invigorating restaurants to hit the Chicago dining scene in quite a while, taking diners on a culinary tour through the largely unexplored island of Macau. The chef behind this Logan Square hot spot is Abe Conlon, who originally hit the local dining circuit with his popular X-marx underground restaurant and can now be found cooking up a delicious storm in the open kitchen at his first brick-and-mortar place. While Conlon cut his teeth on fine French techniques for X-marx, he delved into his own heritage and journeyed through Asia with co-owner Adrienne Lo so as to properly represent the cuisine of Macau, the last European colony in China.

The region was colonized by Portugal, resulting in a melting pot of flavors, textures, ingredients, and preparations. More than just a fusion of Chinese and Portuguese influences, Macanese food draws inspiration from elsewhere in Europe, Latin America, India, and Africa. Growing up in a part-Portuguese family, Conlon was curious to explore this subculture and bring it to Chicago, and the opening of Fat Rice represents a return to form—and his heritage—for a chef who clocked time at places like Chez Asian Bistro in the Dominican Republic and Augustine's in Virginia.

The menu at Fat Rice is a veritable safari of interesting creations unseen elsewhere in the city. The namesake Fat Rice is like paella to the nth degree, pimped out with head-on prawns, pork, sausage, clams, tea-smoked eggs, chicken thighs, and peppers. Along with the eponymous dish, the rest of the menu is designed for sharing as well, and items frequently change. The restaurant has a number of interesting housemade pickles, pot stickers, curry vegetable chamuças (think samosa-style dumpling), rice crisps with pork "floss," and oodles more. Fat Rice is ironically skinny in size, comprising communal tables, several smaller tables, and bar seats overlooking the kitchen, all of which fill up fairly fast.

Above Left: Macanese food is the bill of fare at this red-hot Logan Square restaurant. Photo by Galdones Photography

Top Right: The namesake Fat Rice is a massive portion of paella-like rice with chorizo, duck, pork, linguiça sausage, prawns, clams and tea eggs. Photo by Jason Little

Above Right: With a wide-open kitchen and a cramped, always-packed dining room, the culinary action is on full display. Photo by Galdones Photography

Fat Rice got even fatter in 2016 with the opening of two adjoining businesses, The Bakery by Fat Rice and a clandestine cocktail bar called The Ladies' Room. The former is a sunny, pastoral-hued Chinese-Portuguese bakery with unique items like Mai Tai buns, ube roll cakes, mango milk, and even a bun studded with all the fixings of a Chicago-style hot dog.

The place maintains a fun, energetic vibe, thumping with hip-hop music and the steady hustle of the open kitchen. The drink list is as fascinating and exploratory as the food, with lots of Portuguese and Spanish wines you'd have a hard time finding elsewhere and umeboshi-infused gin and tonics. To dine here is to embark on a gustatory adventure, and you never know what will be presented when you order it. Each item is unique, bursting with unexpected flavors and textures. This is the type of place where you can disregard inhibitions and buckle up for one of the tastiest rides in Chicago.

2957 W Diversey Ave.
773-661-9170
www.eatfatrice.com

Then there's the reservation-only Ladies' Room. Call Fat Rice to reserve a seat and be escorted around the block for access. The window-less, crimson-colored nook feels like a Chinese gambling parlor, lined with Chinese pin-up posters and deep red walls. Cocktails are quite inventive too, featuring items like housemade Malört, housemade "Dr. Pepper," and even a plum brandy made from a recipe courtesy of Fat Rice's Transylvanian janitor.

Top Left: Abraham Conlon and Adrienne Lo are the dynamic duo behind one of Chicago's most original, most popular restaurants. Photo by Galdones Photography

Top Right: Available at brunch and at Fat Rice's adjoining bakery, egg tarts are a little bit sweet, a little bit savory, and entirely perfect. Photo by Jason Little

Bottom: There's much to savor at Fat Rice, from crispy dumplings and innovative cocktails to the namesake Fat Rice dish brimming with seafood and meat. Photo by Jason Little

FLORIOLE CAFE & BAKERY

Croissants, canelés, and tartines, oh my!

Big dreams sometimes start in small tents. Just ask Sandra and Mathieu Holl, the duo behind Lincoln Park's acclaimed Floriole Cafe & Bakery. Between the two of them, they've held a longstanding love for baking, pastry, and everything that comes with it. For Sandra, her background includes studying at San Francisco's California Culinary Academy and clocking time at the city's famed Tartine Bakery, one of the more revered pastry shops in the country. For Mathieu, he has his Parisian upbringing to thank for his engrained respect for quality food, especially pastries and breads. They met in San Francisco, introduced through mutual friends because they both spoke French, before their courtship took them to Chicago.

Together, they brought plenty of passion and prowess to the table in regard to aspiring bakery dreams. When they arrived, they felt that a world-class dining city like Chicago was lagging in terms of pastry and bread, so they set out to change that. For five years, their business consisted of a tiny 10' x 10' tent at Green City Market, where they sold their rustic French-style wares to farmers' market customers, rain or shine. And sometimes snow, because you never know with Chicago weather. While slinging their croissants, scones, and canelés under a tarp, their ultimate goal was of the brick-and-mortar variety.

> "I really loved my baking and pastry classes in culinary school and decided to further explore the idea of working in pastry for my externship," explains Holl of her foray into baking. "I was lucky to land an externship at Tartine and then worked there as a baker for a couple of years."

Top Left: Between the sandwiches, the lustrous salads, the desserts, and the tea, it's easy to make a habit out of dining at Floriole.

Above Left: Sandwiches served on freshly baked bread make for a sensational lunch at this Lincoln Park cafe.

Above Right: The hardest thing about ordering at Floriole is deciding what you want. Or how much is too much.

Finally, that aspiration came true when they opened their gorgeous cafe and bakery not only to serve as home base for all their efforts, but also to expand upon their portfolio exponentially and house some of the city's prettiest and tastiest baked goods. Considering their origin story at a farmers' market, it's apt that locally sourced, seasonal ingredients drive their offerings at Floriole, which runs the gamut from classic desserts like fruit galettes, Basque cake, and strawberry shortcake to composed sandwiches, elegant tartines, rustic breads (the yeasted cornbread is especially revelatory), and much more.

Using produce, meats, and cheeses all from local farmers—many of them their neighbors at the market—the Holls ensure some of the freshest fare in a casual cafe setting, while also bringing their roots and dreams together full circle.

1220 W Webster Ave.
773-883-1313
www.floriole.com

FORBIDDEN ROOT
RESTAURANT & BREWERY

Raise a glass to Chicago's first botanical brewpub

For Forbidden Root, it all began with root beer. In a sense, you can say that this West Town restaurant and brewery, housed in an industrial space formerly home to a movie theater, is rooted in root beer. Founder and self-proclaimed "Rootmaster" Robert Finkel, an expat of the corporate business world and an ardent lover of craft beer, had long been inspired to create a root beer unlike any of the candy-sweet sodas monopolizing the market; he wanted a root beer rich with botanicals and natural herbs and spices.

Thus, Forbidden Root's namesake root beer was created, a complex and malty brew infused with the likes of wintergeen, cassia, sandalwood, cardamom, black pepper, licorice, and cinnamon. It's the domino that set the whole business into action, inspiring a line of botanic beers and beer-friendly food that would eventually become Chicago's first botanical brewery.

Finkel's vision involved tapping into the earliest origins of beer, when forest finds like stems, leaves, roots, and bark were integral parts of brewing, along with spices and flowers like dandelion and ginger. He even goes so far as to source more than one hundred varieties of honey, many of which are aged in barrels for use in dishes and drinks. Aided by head brewer BJ Pichman and executive chef Dan Weiland, Finkel has created one of the most wholly original dining and drinking destinations in the city, a place where guests can pair their Cherrytree Amaro ale with mussels steamed in Wildflower Pale Ale.

1746 W Chicago Ave.
312-929-2202
www.forbiddenroot.com

Top: Housed in a former movie theater, Forbidden Root updates a historic space in West Town. Photo by B. J. Pichman

Bottom: This isn't your average beer food. Try the pork schnitzel sandwich with pickled beet mayo and caraway-cabbage slaw. Photo by B. J. Pichman

Forbidden Root is big on charity. They donate the profits from all of their non-consumable merchandise, with proceeds from shirts and bottle openers going to different causes. At the bar, tap handle 15 is called the "Love Handle." It features a different rotating beer from local breweries and donates $2 from every sale to different organizations.

61

The Mexican restaurant that launched a Rick Bayless empire

One of the most famous chefs in Chicago, nay, the country, first rose to prominence with Frontera Grill. Around these parts, Rick Bayless is a culinary demigod and a venerable ambassador of Mexican cuisine in a city chock full of incredible, authentic, regional Mexican restaurants. It all started with a trip south of the border with his wife, Deann Groen Bayless, in what would turn out to be a recurring and career-orienting travel experience.

Fresh off an extended stay in Mexico, where they spent time eating and researching for Bayless's first book, the pair returned to Chicago with the newfound goal to create a transportive space that felt like travel. Thanks to a design scheme as colorful as a piñata, lively mariachi music, and top-notch Mexican ingredients, their vision

Rick Bayless has quite a few accomplishments under his belt. He's filmed 11 seasons of his popular public television series, Mexico—One Plate at a Time; he's been nominated for a Daytime Emmy; he won the first season of Bravo's Top Chef Masters; he's written nine cookbooks; and he's even performed on stage at the Lookingglass Theatre with his show, Cascabel. The highest acclaim of all, however, came from the country of Mexico itself when the government awarded the chef the Mexican Order of the Aztec Eagle—the most prestigious distinction given to non-natives.

Left: This isn't your average flan. Frontera serves a duo of caramel custards, one made with classic Mexican vanilla and pumpkin, another with raw sugar, pumpkin, and pomegranate. Photo by Frontera

Right: Expect lots and lots of Mexican tequila and mezcal from the bar. Photo by Galdones Photography

came true with Frontera Grill. Now open for more than twenty-five years, an astonishingly long time in the restaurant business, Frontera Grill continues to pack in crowds from near and far—sometimes very, very far.

While neighboring Topolobampo skews towards fine dining, and XOCO specializes in tortas, Frontera Grill is straight-up Mexican food, pristinely executed, Bayless-style. The kitchen uses seasonal, local ingredients, oftentimes custom-grown (or harvested from Bayless's own home garden in Bucktown), to put a Midwestern stamp on bold Mexican flavors. The menu features guacamoles, plenty of raw seafood, tacos, moles, and vivid entrees that draw from traditional Mexican snacks and dishes, elevating them with rigorous attention to detail and a commitment to locality. This is what Bayless-style Mexican food means. From a smoked chicken taquito to Oaxacan-style carne asada, the acclaimed chef recreates traditional south-of-the-border experiences on every plate.

With a chef of Bayless's caliber, there's bound to be some hysteria involved. True to form, all these years later, Frontera Grill remains notoriously difficult to get into. Reservations are accepted, but much of the dining room is saved for walk-ins, and lines can snake out the door.

445 N Clark St.
312-661-1434
www.rickbayless.com/restaurants/frontera-grill

FURIOUS SPOON

The best ramen this side of Tokyo

It seems fated that Shin Thompson would become Chicago's preeminent ambassador for ramen. Much more than a chef hopping aboard the ramen craze that's been sweeping the nation, Thompson has a history with ramen that dates back generations, when his grandfather owned a ramen shop in Hokkaido, Japan. Born in Honolulu, Thompson spent much of his youth in Japan, an experience that would go on to imbue his cooking in unique ways.

Throughout his upbringing and his storied culinary career in Chicago, which included running the acclaimed fine dining restaurant Bonsoiree and Japanese brasserie Kabocha, Thompson brought it all back to ramen with the opening of Furious Spoon.

The bustling Wicker Park noodle shop serves as homage to Thompson's grandfather and his family's ramen roots. A far cry from the cheap ramen noodles popular among college dorm rooms, the stuff at Furious Spoon is the real deal, diligently made by hand using special noodle-pulling equipment shipped from Osaka, simmered in meticulous bowls of broth with accents like delicately poached eggs, succulent pork belly, white pepper chicken, garlic relish, and more. Unlike his previous ventures, which featured broad strokes of fusion fare, Furious Spoon sports a razor-sharp focus that allows Thompson to hone in on what he's great at.

Furious Spoon has been such a hit that Thompson and business partner Anshul Mangal have expanded with new locations in Logan Square, the Loop's Revival Food Hall, and Pilsen. The Logan Square outpost features an expanded beverage program with cocktails on tap and other unique drinks like a nori-infused margarita with togarashi spices.

Top Left: Borrowing inspiration from his grandfather in Japan, chef Shin Thompson oversees the ramen-centric menu at Furious Spoon.

Above Left: It's all about the ramen, featuring homemade noodles and enhancements like tonkotsu broth, poached egg, pork belly, and white pepper chicken.

Above Right: Furious Spoon Logan Square: After amassing acclaim and drawing lines at their Wicker Park original, the Furious Spoon team expanded with a new, larger location in Logan Square.

1571 N Milwaukee Ave.

773-687-8445

furiousramen.com

GEJA'S CAFE

Chicago's most romantic restaurant features fondue made for two

One of the longest-standing restaurants in Chicago is also more romantic than Titanic. There's just something about shareable bowls of fondue in a subterranean, swanky setting that sets the pace for an evening of enchantment. Geja's Cafe is responsible for more engagements than any other restaurant in the city, including that of the owner of the restaurant, Jeff Lawler, who got engaged for the first time at the Lincoln Park fixture. Having owned the restaurant for twenty-three years and helped orchestrate more than three hundred engagements for other couples, the fifty-four-year-old Lawler finally popped the question to his girlfriend on Christmas Day while surrounded by family members. For the couple, the proposal marked a full circle, since they first met at the restaurant in 2012. Though she was living in Columbus, Ohio, at the time, she apparently liked Lawler (and the fondue) so much that she moved to Chicago so they could be together. It's all a testament to Geja's ability to pull heartstrings. For more than fifty years, long after fondue went from

Aside from his own engagement, one of Lawler's fondest memories at Geja's was his first Valentine's Day working at the restaurant. "I opened the front door and saw the long line of guests waiting to dine with us. By 6 p.m., I was quoting people in line a five- to six-hour wait, and most of them said, 'No problem, we expected it,'" he recalls. "These guests returned between 11 p.m. and midnight to start their dinner. To me, that is when I realized this place is truly special."

Top Left: The menu is small but mighty, primarily divided into savory and sweet fondues meant for sharing, featuring dipping items like shrimp, beef, and scallops.

Top Right: For decades, couples have been flocking to Geja's Cafe for romantic servings of fondue.

Bottom Left: With molten chocolate warmed by a portable fire, dessert at Geja's Cafe is basically like making s'mores by a fire.

Bottom Right: Nothing whets the appetite like a crock of melted cheese.

hip trend to kitschy party food, the restaurant has been wooing diners with its time-tested formula of romantic atmosphere and equally romantic dining. Immersed in candlelight and interspersed with intimate tables throughout a labyrinthine floor plan, Geja's is really unlike anything else in Chicago. Guests can indulge in prix fixe dinners focused on savory and sweet fondue bowls, like a bubbling Gruyère cheese fondue with bread and fruit skewers for dipping. There are simmering broth bowls served with the likes of lobster, shrimp, beef tenderloin, and scallops, followed by a rich and creamy chocolate fondue with marshmallows and pound cake. Beginning to end, whether it's a first date or an engagement, there's a lot to love about this place.

340 W Armitage Ave.
773-281-9101
www.gejascafe.com

GENE & GEORGETTI

Chicago's most iconic steakhouse has as much history as it does beef

Not only the oldest steakhouse in Chicago, but one of the city's longest-standing restaurants, Gene & Georgetti has plenty of experience appeasing meat-hungry customers. Founded in 1941 by Gene Michelotti and Alfredo Federighi (his nickname was Georgetti, in case you were puzzled), the old-school steakhouse is the perfect combination of seasoned service and classic cuisine. That's all thanks to the dynamic duo that combined their strengths to open the restaurant together, as Gene managed front of house and Georgetti ran the kitchen.

The two initially met while working in a restaurant shortly after Gene moved to the United States from Lucca, Italy. While Gene was tending bar and Georgetti cooked, they hit it off and developed the idea to go into business together. Along with Georgetti's food, which centered on steaks and other classic chophouse fare like burly wedge salads, shrimp de Jonghe, and veal, it was Gene's omnipresent charm that gave the restaurant its enduring character. He'd famously make the rounds through the dining room, smacking customers on the shoulders and engaging in jovial banter.

Soon enough, word spread to politicians, athletes, and celebrities, and Gene & Georgetti became a local hot spot with service as comforting as the food. The restaurant boasts regulars who have

> "Our philosophy at Gene & Georgetti is to cultivate a diverse team of talented people who give not only their hospitality excellence, but their hearts as well. We believe that when we treat each and every guest like family, they become our family." –Michelle Durpetti, Managing Partner

Top Left: Be it a power lunch, business dinner, or date night, Gene & Georgetti does not disappoint with its classic combo of steaks, sides, wines, and more. Photo by Marcin Cymmer

Top Right: Succulent T-bones, filets, and chops round out the burly menu at Chicago's longest-running steakhouse. Photo by Marcin Cymmer

Bottom Left: Gene & Georgetti is the rare place where salads are as indulgent as the steaks, especially when said salads are studded with shrimp and salami. Photo by Marcin Cymmer

Bottom Right: The River North steakhouse embraces its Italian heritage with colorful dishes like sausage and peppers. Photo by Marcin Cymmer

visited weekly for decades, returning time and again for Gene & Georgetti's eternal hospitality. Although Georgetti died in 1969 and Gene passed in 1989, the restaurant's famous character and time-tested recipes remain in the family, currently operated by Gene's daughter Marion and her husband, Tony Durpetti.

500 N Franklin St.
312-527-3718
www.geneandgeorgetti.com

GIBSONS BAR & STEAKHOUSE

Make like the Rat Pack and dine at the Gold Coast's crown jewel

When it comes to steakhouses in Chicago, Gibsons Bar & Steakhouse is king. Not only is it the most consistently popular steakhouse in a city world famous for its steakhouses, but Gibsons is routinely ranked as the highest-grossing restaurant in the entire city, raking in more than $20 million annually. That's thanks to nearly three decades of top-tier service, high-quality food, and lively atmosphere. Oh, and it doesn't hurt to have a laundry list of celebrity fans. Founded by Steve Lombardo and Hugo Ralli in Chicago's Gold Coast in 1989, at the nexus of an intersection infamously nicknamed the Viagra Triangle for the abundance of gentlemen suitors who frequent the area, Gibsons rapidly emerged as the city's quintessential steakhouse.

It's not the oldest, by any means, but it became the new classic through its thoughtful mix of USDA Gibsons Prime Angus Beef (see sidebar for more on this), old-school cocktails, and unparalleled service so friendly and memorable that waiters start to feel like family friends. And waiters and staffers feel like family toward one another too; several waiters, cooks, and food-runners have been working there for decades. The key to the restaurant's longevity and ceaseless

Gibsons is the only restaurant in the country to have its own designation of Angus beef. Sourced from the northern Midwest, cattle are raised, fed, and processed to very specific standards set by the restaurant, ensuring a product that is consistently tender and flavorful.

Top Left: This is the kind of place where ordering a dirty martini at lunch is highly encouraged.

Above Left: It's meat and potatoes done very, very right at Gibsons Bar & Steakhouse.

Above Right: From Frank Sinatra to Jay-Z, Gibsons boasts many celebrity fans.

appeal is its effortless crowd-pleasing capabilities and timeless sense of comfort. Dining here feels like teleporting to the Rat Pack era of supper clubs, when the dirty martinis were dangerously strong (and the size of lamps), business suits would drink their lunches at the mahogany bar, and convivial calamity in the dining room was the norm during dinner rush.

It's the kind of sprawling, bustling restaurant where meandering rooms and stairwells are lined with autographed photos of celebrity diners; famous fans over the years have included Johnny Depp, Jay-Z and Beyoncé, Michael Jordan, and Celine Dion. Today, Gibsons is more A-list than ever. With an average of six hundred meals served per night, a vast majority of customers order steak as their centerpiece, be it a herculean tomahawk chop, a porterhouse, or W.R.'s Chicago Cut, named for former Chicago food writer William Rice. And when they're through, many save room for Gibsons' notoriously gigantic cakes and pies. To dine here isn't just a typical steakhouse experience; it's participating in an active part of Chicago history.

1028 N Rush St.
312-266-8999
www.gibsonssteakhouse.com

GIRL & THE GOAT

Celeb chef Stephanie Izard showcases a flair for the contemporary at this West Loop hot spot

Since opening in 2010, Girl & The Goat has remained one of the most popular restaurants in Chicago, thanks to the tremendous following behind executive chef and Top Chef winner Stephanie Izard. The chef is legend in Chicago, and while she grew up in Connecticut and attended culinary school in Arizona, the city of her birth came calling, leading her to move back here in 2000 to pursue her cooking career.

Between then and the time she opened her first—and now defunct—restaurant, Scylla, Izard clocked time working alongside some of the country's biggest heavy hitters, like Shawn McClain at Spring and Jean-Georges Vongerichten at Vong. While Scylla earned her cred in the local food community, it wasn't until Izard became the first female winner of *Top Chef* and opened Girl & The Goat that she experienced a tidal wave of success.

Girl & The Goat is likely the most see-and-be-seen restaurant in Chicago in terms of food obsessives. Its widespread acclaim attracts, as if magnetically, tourists and suburbanites as well. As evidenced on *Top Chef*, Izard's food is unique and palate pushing, combining

"I get inspiration from all over. During season, I like to wander the farmers' market to just remind me of different produce that is in season. I love reading about foods from various cultures and taking flavor inspiration. I don't eat out as much as I would like to now that I have a baby, but finding fun little hidden spots when I travel is always good inspiration." –Stephanie Izard

Dark and whimsical, like something out of a Tim Burton fantasy, Girl & the Goat sports a unique motif unlike anything in Chicago. Photo by Anthony Tahlier

flavors and textures in Willy Wonka-esque ways, resulting in dishes both delicious and memorable. Izard has a way with rustic preparations, taking homey ingredients and presenting them in invigorating new ways. Take, for example, the green beans with fish sauce vinaigrette and cashews; the shishito peppers with Parmesan, sesame, and miso; or escargot ravioli with bacon and tamarind-miso sauce. She's also known for whole-animal cookery, employing an in-house butcher to break down entire beasts for use throughout her menu (as in the wood oven-roasted pig face with egg, tamarind, cilantro, red wine-maple, and potato stix). Girl & The Goat was one of the first restaurants to charge for bread, but it's worth it. Flavors change daily and vary from "fat bread" (made with smoked duck fat) to pretzel bread, and even a jumbo pig-in-a-blanket. All breads are made across the street at Little Goat Bread. The place is consistently packed from 5 p.m. until close every day of the week, and while reservations are difficult to come by, they keep a wait-list for walk-ins, and the bar area is always up for grabs too. The industrial-style space is large, rambunctious, and loud. At peak hours, it can feel like a rock concert. Much of the seating is communal, and food comes out of the kitchen at random—whenever something's ready, that's when you eat it. And you'll eat it happily.

809 W Randolph St.
312-492-6262
www.girlandthegoat.com

Izard's success has seen her expansion throughout the West Loop, starting with Little Goat Diner across the street. The all-day/late-night comfort food mecca features innovative and playful twists on nostalgia items, like a Spanish omelet with masa chips or a riff on a sloppy Joe made with goat meat and rosemary slaw on a squash roll. In 2016, she added a Chinese restaurant nearby called Duck Duck Goat, again featuring novel twists on staples like crab rangoon, scallion pancakes, and noodles tossed with goat sausage.

Top: One of the most perpetually packed restaurants on Restaurant Row, Stephanie Izard's hot spot still fills reservations months in advance. Photo by Anthony Tahlier

Bottom Left: Stephanie Izard's inventive menu is ever-changing, featuring offbeat combos like escargot ravioli, green beans and fish sauce vinaigrette, and duck tongues with tuna and black beans. Photo by Anthony Tahlier

Bottom Right: A standout dish on the menu since day one, wood-oven roasted pig face comes with a sunny-side egg, tamarind, cilantro, red wine-maple, and crunchy potato "stix." Photo by Anthony Tahlier

GREEN ZEBRA

Serving up vegetarian food since before it was cool

Green Zebra is a restaurant on a mission. Especially in a city like Chicago, where the meat-and-potatoes cliché has long reigned supreme, it took guts to open a restaurant focused entirely on vegetables—especially in 2004, long before the city's current spate of veg-heavy restaurants helped normalize the philosophy. Shawn McClain is a brave pioneer in that regard. Since opening day, the chef/owner has kept his focus on the purity of vegetables, omitting meat in favor of pristine produce such as golden beet salad with watermelon radish, kabocha squash and white miso soup, rutabaga dumplings, and chilled sōmen noodles with hearts of palm and papaya.

This is a place where a tomato tastes like it's supposed to—a tomato. And in its earlier days, such places were an anomaly. So what's the secret to success for McClain and company? Green Zebra may be a vegetarian restaurant, sure, but it removes any tofu-heavy stigma through its graceful, seasonal approach to vegetable-focused cuisine. Rather than imitate meat dishes (no "chickin" or "tofurkey" here), the restaurant showcases the versatility of seasonal vegetables and how they can play on the same grand stage as meatier fine-dining destinations. You need not be a vegetarian to enjoy a meal at Green Zebra.

This is a place with haute small plates featuring locally sourced seasonal ingredients in unique combinations. If omnivores come

"Cooking a vegetable-focused menu is important to me because it makes me happy to go to the Green City Market and see great produce there," explains Chapman. "Working with local farms is also important to me, and it's the basis for vegetable-focused food."

Top Left: Green Zebra has been a veggie pioneer in the Midwest since 2004. Photo by Green Zebra

Above left: Just because vegetables are front-and-center doesn't mean the food isn't rich. Take this farm egg with buttery toasted bread, for instance. Photo by Green Zebra

Above right: Dishes like this heirloom tomato salad showcase the natural artistry of seasonal ingredients. Photo by Green Zebra

in with an open mind, they'll be pleasantly satiated, especially with Green Zebra's mushroom-focused dishes, packed with meaty umami flavor. It also helps that the restaurant is by no means vegan and does not shy away from butter, eggs, cream, and other enriching ingredients. Another focal point is the artistry involved in plating, showing off veggies in gorgeous new ways that'll make you forget all about meat and seafood. Nowadays, more than a decade in and still going strong, chef de cuisine David Chapman mans the kitchen as McClain spends most of his time in Las Vegas, spreading the Midwestern food gospel at his restaurant Sage. For Chapman, the role is the culmination of a long-standing dream. He still vividly recalls everything he ate at his first meal at Shawn McClain's Spring in 2004, and it drove him to work with the acclaimed chef.

The atmosphere at Green Zebra is as refreshingly modern and minimalist as the food, like a vegetable art gallery—where diners eat most of the art. Mission accomplished.

1460 W Chicago Ave.
312-243-7100
www.greenzebrachicago.com

HEAVEN ON SEVEN

A classic ode to New Orleans seven stories above the Loop

One of the most important names in Chicago food, Jimmy Bannos has become the foremost ambassador of New Orleans-style food in the Midwest at his legendary restaurant Heaven on Seven. A third-generation restaurateur, Bannos hails from a family that is exalted in Chicago, ever since the chef transformed his New Garland Coffee Shop into the decades-old Cajun eatery in the heart of the Loop. The restaurant industry has been Bannos's life as long as he can remember.

Along with his brother George, he grew up cleaning tables and washing dishes in his parents' restaurants. In 1980, it was time to carve out his own path, with a cafe on the seventh floor of downtown's historic Garland Building. It began as his version of a cozy, casual neighborhood coffee shop, where he was joined by his brother and parents in greeting guests and making the space a welcoming environment for all. Five years later, after delving further and further into his love for New Orleans cuisine and culture, Bannos rebranded the space into Heaven on Seven.

Stepping off the elevator and into Heaven is a wholly transportive experience that feels like stepping off an airplane and into the French Quarter, where colorful beads and masks adorn the restaurant and shelves of Cajun hot sauce line the dining room walls. Bannos's food is a culmination of decades of passion for Louisiana recipes and

The Bannos legacy has never been stronger, as Jimmy's son and fourth-generation restaurateur Jimmy Bannos Jr. mans the kitchen at The Purple Pig, a wildly popular Mediterranean restaurant and wine bar nearby on Michigan Avenue.

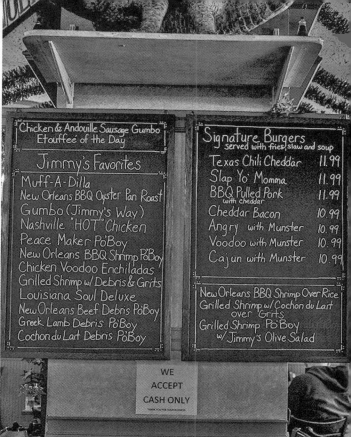

Chicken & Andouille Sausage Gumbo
Etouffée of the Day

Jimmy's Favorites

Muff-A-Dilla
New Orleans BBQ Oyster Pan Roast
Gumbo (Jimmy's Way)
Nashville "HOT" Chicken
Peace Maker Po'Boy
New Orleans BBQ Shrimp Po'Boy
Chicken Voodoo Enchiladas
Grilled Shrimp w/ Debris & Grits
Louisiana Soul Deluxe
New Orleans Beef Debris Po'Boy
Greek Lamb Debris Po'Boy
Cochon du Lait Debris Po'Boy

Signature Burgers
served with fries, slaw and soup

Texas Chili Cheddar   11.99
Slap Yo' Momma   11.99
BBQ Pulled Pork   11.99
  with cheddar
Cheddar Bacon   10.99
Angry with Munster   10.99
Voodoo with Munster   10.99
Cajun with Munster   10.99

New Orleans BBQ Shrimp Over Rice
Grilled Shrimp w/ Cochon du Lait
          over Grits
Grilled Shrimp Po'Boy
  w/ Jimmy's Olive Salad

WE
ACCEPT
CASH ONLY

Top Left: The man behind the kitchen magic at Heaven on Seven: Jimmy Bannos. Photo by Tuan Huyhn

Above Left: Heaven on Seven features some of the finest po'boys in Chicago, like this fried shrimp version with Cajun slaw and honey-jalapeño dressing.

Above Right: Generations continue to frequent the restaurant for authentic po'boys, gumbo, BBQ shrimp, and lots more. Photo by Tuan Huyhn

countless trips to the Crescent City. His menu features Southern comfort foods galore, from fried green tomatoes with remoulade to fiery grilled andouille sausage with Creole mustard, bracing bowls of jambalaya, fried catfish, oyster po'boys, and rice pudding that Bannos makes from his late mother's recipe.

111 N Wabash Ave.
312-263-6443
www.heavenonseven.com

HONEY BUTTER FRIED CHICKEN

Farm-fresh ingredients get some serious comfort food treatment in Avondale

It all started at an underground restaurant, where diners cleaned their plates of honey butter-slathered fried chicken and raved to the chefs so much that they began to toy with the idea of a non-underground restaurant. The idea for Honey Butter Fried Chicken, Avondale's gloriously indulgent temple of chef-driven comfort food, was born out of Sunday Dinner Club, an in-the-know quasi-restaurant still operated by Christine Cikowski and Joshua Kulp.

Nowadays, the two dining concepts are a symbiotic pair, with Sunday Dinner Club operating out of an upstairs space above Honey Butter Fried Chicken, but for years the former ran as a secretive invitation-only dinner party-inspired experience out of apartments in Chicago. This is where co-chefs Cikowski and Kulp fully forged their partnership and developed the idea to open a full-fledged restaurant directly inspired by the most popular meal served at Sunday Dinner. Honey Butter Fried Chicken represents a culmination of more than ten years of underground dinners and ceaseless commitment to local sourcing and farmer's markets (Cikowski and Kulp formerly ran a burger stand at Green City Market to much fanfare and are still avid shoppers at Chicago's largest farmers' market).

Cikowski and Kulp still operate Sunday Dinner Club on days and evenings when Honey Butter Fried Chicken is closed. The in-the-know concept is such that people get added to their mailing list at events or by attending with friends. Each dinner centers on a specific theme, be it Italian, Chinese, cassoulet, or coq au vin.

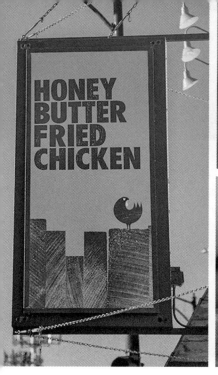

Above Left: Follow your nose (and the bright yellow sign) to fried chicken heaven in Avondale.

Top Right: You gotta go on Thursdays for the once-a-week fried chicken nachos, piled with pimento cheese, tortilla chips, lime crema, corn pico de gallo, and candied jalapeños.

Above Right: "The OG" sandwich features fried chicken strips, candied jalapeño mayo, and crunchy slaw on a buttery bun. Credit Tim Musho

Here, they use responsibly raised chickens from Miller Amish Farms in Indiana that are brined, battered, and fried in trans-fat-free canola oil. Along with seasonal vegetables for sides, honey for the butter, and cornmeal for cornbread muffins, each and every ingredient meets their rigorous standards for locality and sustainability. Although the act of smearing honey butter on fried chicken seems excessive at first, it really takes the food to the next level. Ever since the chefs first tried it at Sunday Dinner, urging diners not to be shy about trying it too, it's been a smash hit. From underground restaurant to the forefront of Chicago's fried chicken scene, Honey Butter Fried Chicken is the little dream that accomplished it all.

3361 N Elston Ave.
773-478-4000
www.honeybutter.com

HOOSIER MAMA PIE COMPANY

Americana desserts don't get any more wholesome than this

Big things often have small beginnings. This is certainly true of Hoosier Mama Pie Company, which originated as a homey pastime in Indiana before blossoming into one of Chicago's most adored pastry destinations.

It's all courtesy of Paula Haney, a chef who first got a taste for pie when making desserts with her mom in their home kitchen in the Hoosier State. Considering that apple pie was the first thing she learned to make, it resonated and stuck with her for years, even through journalism school and stints in fine dining restaurants. It always came back to pie. That vivid memory of slicing apples as a child, transfixed by the contrasting flavors and textures of the all-American classic, is something Haney valued as a source of comfort.

As an adult in Chicago, when she would get home late from work, it's this ultimate comfort food that soothed her most after clocking long hours at places like Trio, where she helped prepare desserts for multi-course tasting menus at the now-defunct Evanston institution. While fine dining certainly helped refine her culinary skills, pie retained a special place in her heart, and it quickly evolved from something she would do as an at-home hobby into a burgeoning business as a vendor at Green City Market, working out of shared

For those looking to embrace their inner Hoosier Mama, Haney's cookbook is available on Amazon or at Hoosier Mama's West Town cafe. The Hoosier Mama Book of Pie covers everything you need to know to bake the perfect pie, from dough in chapter one to quiches and hand pies.

Top Left: Paula Haney is the "Mama" at Hoosier Mama, taking her lifelong love for pies and baking to the hungry masses. Photo by Rob Warner

Bottom Left: The pint-sized pie shop is always filled with alluring flavors like chocolate cream, pumpkin, and the namesake Hoosier sugar cream, a rich and caramel-scented variation. Photo by Rob Warner

Above Right: Even something as iconic and straightforward as sweet potato pie gets the next-level treatment at Hoosier Mama, with its silky-smooth custard texture and glazed pecans for crunch. Photo by Dan Zemens

kitchen space to develop recipes. Before she knew it, Haney had a bit of a cult following on her hands, with enough customer demand to merit opening a storefront. She eventually did so with an adorably quaint bake shop in West Town, a cozy nook with only a few tiny tables and the general soul-soothing sensation of dining in someone's cottage.

For Haney, the shop represents a full-circle return to the homey environment that first got her hooked on pie. And you'll be hooked too, whether it's on Hoosier Mama's perfect apple pie (the only pie available year round, due to rightful customer demand), pumpkin pie, berry pies, or more offbeat novelties like silky orange cream or the Fat Elvis, made with chocolate, bananas, and peanut butter in a graham cracker crust. Nowadays, while Haney has branched out with a cafe in Evanston and even a cookbook, her folksy and familial roots remain front and center at Chicago's preeminent pie shop.

1618 W Chicago Ave.
312-243-4846
www.hoosiermamapie.com

Belgian beer and habit-forming mussels in cozy Andersonville environs

Long before gastropubs swept the nation and monopolized beer-and-food culture, there was Hopleaf. The dream of Michael Roper, a longtime bar industry vet from Detroit, Hopleaf represented an opportunity to come into his own in his adopted hometown. After owning a bar in Detroit for several years, culminating in the building burning down, he made the move to Chicago and bided his time looking for the right spot to make his mark.

When Roper and his wife Louise Molnar opened Hopleaf in 1992, light-years ago in restaurant industry time, it took shape in a former Swedish dive bar. Although the bar was a far cry from its roots, Roper purchased the space, added a new bar, put in windows, and carved out a new niche in the historically Swedish neighborhood of Andersonville.

That niche is Belgian beer, and they've got quite an impressive roster on tap and by the bottle. In fact, Hopleaf has perhaps more bottled Belgian beers than any bar this side of Brussels, including numerous rare beers, some Gueuzes, and large-format beers with sizes going up to Jereboam, a three-liter goliath. Currently, their lineup includes upwards of 70 draft lines, eight wines on tap, and more than 300 bottles. Drinking here is basically tantamount to a lesson in the Belgian language, but purely for fun. Those who prefer domestic beers have plenty of options as well, with a number of American craft brews on tap and in bottles.

The name Hopleaf is an homage to Roper's heritage. It's a pale ale made by England's defunct Simonds Brewery, long renowned for supplying beer to the British fleet as early as the 1700s. There's still a brewery making the ale on Malta to this day, and Roper is a frequent visitor.

Left: Belgian beer is the name of the game at this Andersonville gem. Photo by Bradley Kirouac

Right: Hopleaf's ever-inventive food menu raises the bar on beer food, like this duck Reuben sandwich with cranberry-cream cheese spread, sauerkraut, and Emmenthaler cheese. Photo by Grant Kessler

The phone book-sized beer menus can be intimidating for some, so the bar helps guests navigate it by providing meticulous descriptions for all beers. It's also nifty that every beer comes in its own distinct glass, since each variety benefits differently from glass shape in order to maximize flavor and aroma.

Don't stop at the beers because the Belgian-inspired food menu provides some of the most comforting bar food in the city. Mussels—available steamed in white wine or white ale, in half or full portions—and frites are crazy popular. Chef Ben Sheagren has a knack for hearty, beer-friendly fare, with a particular affinity for meat. As a dexterous charcuterie master, his cured meats and applewood-smoked brisket sell like hot cakes.

Though Hopleaf has expanded into the adjacent building, effectively doubling their seating capacity, you'll still run into more elbows than in a mosh pit. The bar does not take reservations, and wait times frequently stretch over an hour. The fact that this is a bar, with plenty of beer to drink while you wait, alleviates the process though. The smaller upstairs space is less stifling, and a back patio during warm weather offers a bit more wiggle room. Roper and Molnar have come a long way since first getting into the bar business, and it's safe to say, some 20-plus years in, they've successfully found their niche in Hopleaf.

5148 N Clark St.
773-334-9851
www.hopleafbar.com

HOTCHOCOLATE

Dessert steals the show at Mindy Segal's beloved Bucktown staple

Mindy Segal is so much more than a pastry chef and an award-winning, nationally lauded pastry chef at that. No, the chef/owner of Bucktown's venerable HotChocolate is a rock star. She's a dynamo of a businesswoman. She's a powerhouse force that strikes fear in some and the utmost admiration and inspiration in so many others. With apt nicknames like "Chicago's pastry queen," Segal rightly has an intimidating reputation, and she's got the background to prove it.

Growing up in Chicago's North Shore, she would routinely get into trouble and break curfew, but cooking was always a calming outlet and something that came naturally. It apparently impressed her parents enough since they're investors in her restaurant. She attended culinary school at Kendall College in Chicago and went on to work under some of the most prestigious names in town, including Charlie Trotter, Judy Contino, and Michael Kornick. The latter is where she really rose to local acclaim as Kornick's pastry chef

Although Segal scrapped initial plans for a bakery in Logan Square, she's expanded her repertoire quite nicely in the past few years. This includes her first cookbook, *Cookie Love*, and a casual cafe in the Loop's Revival Food Hall, where she supplies baked goods and hot chocolate. Then there's her much-ballyhooed work with marijuana edibles. Segal developed a line of products for medical marijuana dispensaries in Illinois, including milk chocolate peanut brittle, PB&J caramel, and vanilla-bourbon-butterscotch candies.

Left: Bags of hot chocolate mix and other take-home items are available by the front counter. Photo by Scott Shigley

Center: Come for the desserts, stay because you're in a food coma. Photo by Anthony Tahlier

Right: Whether it's keeping cozy in the wintertime or basking in the glow of summer, HotChocolate is a Bucktown fixture all year round. Photo by Scott Shigley

at his eponymous mk The Restaurant. When she left to open her own restaurant in 2005, she channeled years of ambition, angst, and rebellion into pure drive.

HotChocolate represented her opportunity to shine on her own terms, albeit highly perfectionistic terms that meant baking batch after batch of cookies until they were absolutely perfect. As the name suggests, HotChocolate is a temple of desserts, but it's also so much more than that. This is a restaurant with enough gusto to stand up to the best dining spots in Chicago.

It began as an outlet to showcase her sweets, but Segal also wanted to make the restaurant welcoming to all. Thus, despite the dessert-centric name, HotChocolate traffics in lunch, dinner, and brunch, making it a solid dining destination for any craving. That being said, Segal's pastries are worthy of the national accolades and awards she's amassed, including that of Outstanding Pastry Chef from the James Beard Foundation. Her desserts are often seasonally inspired, composed with pristine ingredients and meticulous, modern preparations, like a neo peach Melba, petite baked Alaskas with various fruity fillings, and apple butter cannoli.

While a good chunk of the dessert menu highlights seasonally available ingredients, Segal also treads heavily in nostalgia, offering her take on brioche doughnuts, kettle corn, cookies, milkshakes, ice creams, and of course, hot chocolate. Obviously hot chocolate is a requisite, available in flavors such as chai, Mexican hot chocolate, dark hot chocolate, and black & tan made with hot fudge and medium hot chocolate. Each version is thick and rich, bedecked with fluffy housemade marshmallows.

Following a renovation in 2012, HotChocolate's savory menus took a turn toward more casual, comfort food-focused fare. Menus follow a pretty traditional appetizer-entree-dessert format, with plates such as housemade soft pretzels, mac & cheese, panzanella salad, eggplant Parmesan, crab cakes, and a particularly popular hamburger. Lunch is more leisurely and sandwich-focused, while brunch offers an expansive array of rotating pastries, quiche, French toast, tartlets, and hash. The renovated HotChocolate has a modern industrial feel, with lots of dark, earthy tones. The elongated space stretches back along the bar to an open kitchen.

It's undoubtedly been a long, often bumpy road getting here, but Segal finally has the fully realized restaurant of her dreams, and considering the accolades and successes that have rained in, it proves that drive pays off.

1747 N Damen Ave.
773-489-1747
www.hotchocolatechicago.com

Top Left: On your way out the door, you'd be wise to pick up some cookies to go. Photo by Anthony Tahlier

Top Right: The industrial-chic space is home base for Mindy Segal's acclaimed desserts and pastries. Photo by Scott Shigley

Above Left: The restaurant's ever-changing dessert menu features elaborate creations ranging from brûléed mini pies and chestnut blondies to dark chocolate gâteau. Photo by Anthony Tahlier

Above Right: After undergoing a remodel, HotChocolate sports a comfortable industrial-chic dining room complete with a long and lively bar area. Photo by Scott Shigley

From rotating guest chefs to a hidden sushi restaurant, this is fine dining that's full of surprises

Intro isn't so much a standard upscale restaurant as it is an incubator of talent and an ever-changing chameleon of cuisines and styles. When Lettuce Entertain You Enterprises shuttered its revered fine-dining fixture L20, diners across the country waited with bated breath to see what would replace it and what could possibly fill those storied shoes. Not only did they fill them, but they went a size up with Intro, a restaurant hinged on a totally unique concept that entails welcoming chefs-in-residence and performing such thorough menu changes that each iteration is tantamount to opening a brand new restaurant.

The highfalutin experiment all started in 2015, when Los Angeles-based chef CJ Jacobson became Intro's first chef-in-residence. At the time, this meant that Intro would feature a menu and design scheme by a different chef every few months. It offered a unique opportunity for Chicagoans to sample the work of different chefs, up-and-coming or otherwise, from different locales.

The concept worked the other way around too—it afforded visiting chefs the chance to get acquainted with Chicago. This is the pivotal point that has made Intro so successful; not only is the restaurant able to continually evolve and adapt, but it's also turned into a culinary ambassador for Chicago. After Jacobson's stint came to an end, the acclaimed chef and *Top Chef* vet remained in Chicago and wound up moving here full time. He opened Ēma, a contemporary restaurant with Mediterranean and Middle Eastern accents, in 2016.

Similarly, Intro nabbed Stephen Gillanders as its fourth chef-in-residence. Another Los Angeles transplant, the chef cooked up Intro's first a la carte menu with a focus on contemporary Asian cuisine inspired by his travels through countries like Japan, Vietnam, and the Philippines. His reception was so successful that he stayed on as the restaurant's first executive chef, a position he holds today, working alongside various chefs-in-residence to co-pilot their menus.

Top: Stephen Gillanders gives beef and broccoli the gourmet treatment. Photo by Anjali Pinto

Bottom: Tuna pizza off chef-in-residence Hisanobu Osaka's menu. Photo by Anjali Pinto

Another unique component to Intro is the separate sushi restaurant tucked away behind the kitchen. Naoki Sushi quickly emerged as one of the best sushi spots in Chicago after it opened in early 2016, featuring bracingly fresh fish in a cool, clandestine environment that guests can only access by walking through Intro's working kitchen.

The concept is something distinct not merely for Chicago, but for the country at large. Not only has Intro lured talent from other cities and added to Chicago's dining scene as a whole, but it also pairs chefs together and combines visions for one-of-a-kind menus, from a vegetable-focused degustation by Jessica Largey to Hisanobu Osaka's eclectic ode to Japanese-inspired trattorias. There's no other dining experience in town quite like Intro, a restaurant where diners never know quite what to expect, except for the fact that everything is sure to be a pleasant surprise.

2300 N Lincoln Park W
773-868-0002
introchicago.com

IPSENTO

Coffee goes farm-to-mug at these hip cafes

From cardamom lattes and Campari cocktails to doughnuts made with house-milled ancient grains, it's instantly clear that Ipsento is not your standard coffee shop. The cafe's history jives handily with its name, a combo of two Latin words that translate to "self discovery." Indeed, Ipsento's path from its opening in 2006 to its current standing, with two locations in Bucktown, has been a colorful journey of discovery and progress.

The shop's original owners, Jeremy and Rachel Smith, gave the company to their church when they opted to start a family. A few months later, the church handed it to current owners Tim and Mandi Taylor, who have guided Ipsento's journey from comfortable coffee shop to one of the most original caffeine fixes in Chicago. The Taylors were well equipped too, having operated a direct-trade coffee importing and roasting business prior to taking over Ipsento.

Naturally, coffee here is of the utmost quality, sourced from sustainable farms across the globe, roasted in their roasting facility a block away, and offered alongside an inventive menu of sandwiches (try the Ernest Hemingway with salmon, egg, capers, and cream cheese on a croissant) and lattes. Their namesake latte is a spiced, aromatic brew of coconut milk, honey, and cayenne.

In 2016, Ipsento's journey took them down the street with a new outpost in a chic industrial space that allowed the owners to expand their vision to more food and drinks. This includes mini doughnuts made from sweet potatoes and house-milled kamut, an ancient nourishing grain with Mesopotamian origins. By night, they morph the coffee bar into a different kind of bar, slinging contemporary riffs on classic cocktails like old-fashioneds and Negronis, alongside a menu of charcuterie, cheese, and other snacky items. The goal was to extend their craft beverage focus beyond coffee, extending to cocktails, beer, whiskey, wine, and sake. It's all part of a seamless, organic progression for a company that's always been on a journey.

Top: Thanks to husband-wife duo Tim and Mandi Taylor, Ipsento has grown from a fledgling shop to one of the city's finest names in coffee.

Above Left: At Ipsento, the namesake coconut-honey-cayenne combo comes in both latte and doughnut form.

Above Center: Made from sweet potatoes and an ancient grain called kamut, Ipsento's mini doughnuts are unlike anything else in Chicago.

Above Right: The shop's owners source coffee from sustainable farms all over the world to ensure the best possible brews.

Western Ave:
2035 N Western Ave.
773-904-8177

Milwaukee Ave:
1813 N Milwaukee Ave.
872-206-8697

www.ipsento.com

A veritable village of transportive Italian restaurants in the Loop

In recent years, Chicago has seen an explosion of haute Italian restaurants all over town. But long before the cuisine became the de facto dining trend, there was Italian Village, a bona fide wonderland of comfort food reigning over the Loop like a castle of red sauce and pasta.

The palatial restaurant complex dates back to 1927, when a young immigrant from Florence named Alfredo Capitanini achieved his grandest ambitions of opening a restaurant of his own. After earning money by washing dishes and cooking in local restaurants, Capitanini was finally able to christen The Village, a vast restaurant with an equally sprawling menu that drew inspiration from various regions of Italy. Along with Capitanini's signature dish, chicken Vesuvio, the menu ran the gamut from fettuccini Alfredo and pizza to veal saltimbocca and eggplant Parmigiana. The restaurateur also decorated the dining room with its signature Tuscan night sky mural, twinkling with stars and awash with blue, along with a colorful, roving floor plan that transports guests to an al fresco Italian villa. The crowd-pleasing restaurant quickly caught on, and soon Chicagoans were clamoring for seats in the downtown hot spot.

Even the city's most gastronomic gangster, Al Capone, is said to have dined here. By 1955, The Village entered a new era. Capitanini's kids were working at the restaurant, helping create a second restaurant in the same building called La Cantina. While The Village is boisterous and convivial, La Cantina feels more like a subdued wine cellar, outfitted with old wine crates, iron gates, and a dizzying array of vintage wine bottles. The family didn't stop here though.

Wine is a big deal at Italian Village. The collective restaurants boast a wine cellar filled with mostly Italian varietals, with more than 35,000 bottles on hand at any given time.

Top Left: Thanks to the freshest, most vibrant ingredients, the most classic creations are endlessly exciting at Italian Village.

Top Right: Crispy calamari doesn't get any better than the version you'll find here.

Bottom Left: Italian Village is as prominent and iconic in the Loop as any of the city's historic theaters and destinations.

Bottom Right: For decades, the restaurant has been transporting guests to the moonlit streets of Florence through its gorgeous vintage design.

In 1961, they added The Florentine Room (now called Vivere), an homage to the elder Capitanini's homeland on the ground floor. The upscale restaurant helped catapult Italian food, especially regional fare from Florence, into the local culinary spotlight in a bold new way. People were finally viewing Italian food as having the same fine-dining potential as other high-end destinations. Though Alfredo has passed, his family legacy lives on today and his dreams have exceeded his wildest expectations. Nowadays, third-generation owner Gina Capitanini keeps tradition alive at the most impactful Italian restaurant in Chicago.

71 W Monroe St.
312-332-7005
www.italianvillage-chicago.com

JOE'S SEAFOOD, PRIME STEAK & STONE CRAB

A Miami classic gets a Midwestern makeover in River North

Joe's Stone Crab is the story of the little crab shack that could. One of the most perpetually popular restaurants in Chicago has come a long way since its Miami Beach origins in the early 1900s, when Hungary-born Joe Weiss moved to Florida for asthma issues (New York City's air wasn't cutting it) and arranged a few seats and tables on his front porch to serve food to hungry passersby. His reputation for Florida stone crab spoke for itself, and the customers kept coming, more and more over the years. In 2000, the Weiss family partnered with Lettuce Entertain You Enterprises, one of the most successful and visible restaurant groups in Chicago, presenting them with the opportunity to take their food and hospitality to the next level. Officially transforming into Joe's Seafood, Prime Steak & Stone Crab for the Chicago opening, the restaurant brought a ritzy taste of Miami Beach to River North, with slick tuxedo-clad servers manning the boisterous dining rooms and delivering platters of crab claws and thick slices of key lime pie to diners so happy they all look like they're on vacation. To this day, the glossy Chicago offshoot is as much an original as the humble Miami mothership.

Naturally, stone crab is the bread and butter of the restaurant. These are crustaceans plucked from the Gulf of Mexico and harvested one claw at a time. They're interactive, too, as each claw gets cracked at the table to reveal the succulent meat inside.

Top: Florida stone crab claws, the ingredient that built a legacy. Photo by Anjali Pinto

Above Left: Considering its beachside Miami roots, it's no surprise that Joe's is expert at fresh seafood. Photo by Anjali Pinto

Above Center: When Joe's came to Chicago, the company put its Midwestern stamp on the storied brand by adding stellar steaks to the repertoire. Photo by Anjali Pinto

Above Right: Since expanding the brand in Chicago, Joe's has gone well beyond crab claws with other delicious items like fried chicken. Photo by Anjali Pinto

60 E. Grand Ave.
312-379-5637
www.joes.net/chicago

The Graziano family tradition is alive and well at this old-school Italian market and sub shop

When it comes to Italian delis and markets in Chicago, it doesn't get more authentic and soulful than J. P. Graziano. In the heart of Restaurant Row, amidst some of the most attention-grabbing restaurants in the country, J. P. Graziano is an old-school diversion, rich with Italian delicacies and the best sandwiches this side of Rome.

The perfect example of quality over quantity, this time-tested eatery doesn't peddle a lot of items, but what they do offer is top-notch. J. P. Graziano got its start way back in 1937, when the Graziano patriarch, Vincenzo (though he went by J. P. because it sounded more "American"), moved from an Italian town called Bagheria to the United States, initially in pursuit of a girl he was pining for.

But since not all love stories end well, Vincenzo found out the girl was already spoken for. Fortunately, he happened to bump into an uncle who was also bound for America, and he convinced Vincenzo to join him in opening a butcher shop in New York City. After his uncle passed away, Vincenzo migrated to Chicago, following the surge of Sicilians settling down in the Midwest. It was here where he opened a wholesale market on Randolph Street in the West Loop, well before the area became the dining mecca it is today.

For many decades, his shop operated as wholesale only, serving the city's thriving Italian expats. Fast-forward to today, and fourth-generation owner Jim Graziano has implemented some great changes. As Randolph Street evolved into the restaurant juggernaut it is today, Jim shifted the focus of the store more toward retail, in order to entice some of the hungry passersby. Now, in addition to imported Italian groceries, which have been a Graziano staple for more than seventy years, the shop offers made-to-order sandwiches, and they're among the best in town.

Made with the best ingredients, including imported Italian meats and cheeses and bread from nearby D'Amato's Bakery, the sandwiches are masterpieces. They're a buck or two more than those

Left: Anatomy of a perfect Chicago lunch: Italian sub, spicy giardiniera, fizzy soda, and some crunchy chips. Photo by Alain Milotti

Center: For the better part of a century, the Graziano family has been an integral part of Chicago's Italian food scene.

Right: You'd be remiss in passing over J.P Graziano's incomparable cannolis, topped off with syrupy Italian cherries. Photo by Alain Milotti

at comparable sandwich shops, but they contain more meat, and the quality is second to none. The bread takes the whole thing over the top, combining the perfect foundation of crunchy crust and fluffy interior. The Italian sandwich is mandatory, stuffed with enough cured Italian meats to feed a family. On subsequent visits, venture further with other items like the Mr. G (the house specialty loaded with imported provolone, hot soppressata, prosciutto di Parma, Volpi Genoa salami, truffle mustard balsamic vinaigrette, hot oil, marinated Roman-style artichokes, fresh basil, lettuce, red wine vinegar, and oregano), the tuna sandwich, or the veggie sandwich. Customers can also supplement sandwiches with giardiniera, artichokes, and sun-dried tomatoes as they please.

Be warned: once the bread is out for the day, sandwiches are done. They occasionally run out before closing, so get there sooner rather than later. The familial nature and history of the place are palpable and warming, and especially considering the nostalgic old-school vibe, it's a breath of fresh air.

901 W Randolph St.
312-666-4587
www.jpgraziano.com

KATHERINE ANNE CONFECTIONS

Chicago's very own chocolate wonderland in Logan Square

Everybody's gotta start somewhere, even Chicago's reigning queen of chocolate. For Katherine Duncan, owner of Katherine Anne Confections, that meant developing an obsession with chocolate truffles, and caramels at an early age during the holiday season, when she would make sweets with her family. Each year, they'd hone recipes and expand their dessert portfolio, using cream from her family's cows to craft caramels.

It's a tradition Duncan continued when she moved in with her now-husband. Every Christmas, she'd make more and more truffles and caramels, to the point where she developed a reputation for them and people started placing orders. Soon enough, truffles evolved from Christmas pastime to a part-time job, as Duncan found herself filling orders after work. In 2006, she formally founded Katherine Anne Confections, selling her wares at local shops, cafes, markets, and events. Over the years, she expanded her repertoire exponentially, developing new flavors for truffles, caramels, and marshmallows by drawing inspiration from classic flavor pairings, cocktails, and even by dining at restaurants and envisioning that cherry and Earl Grey tea would make for a great truffle.

In 2012, Duncan opened a storefront for her business in Logan Square, providing a permanent place where customers could purchase her habit-forming creations. It also afforded her the opportunity to add truffle-infused hot chocolates to her menu, rich and fudgy winter warmers that make regular hot cocoa taste like water by comparison. She serves her hot chocolate with fluffy housemade marshmallows in various flavors like cinnamon-sugar and chai tea, each one designed to pair perfectly with a particular drink. Nowadays, with Duncan firmly established as Chicago's

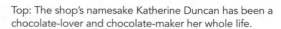

Top: The shop's namesake Katherine Duncan has been a chocolate-lover and chocolate-maker her whole life.

Bottom: Like the Willy Wonka factory, Katherine Anne confectioners are constantly stirring up new ideas and flavors for truffles, like goat cheese-walnut, chai-coconut and even Manhattan cocktail truffles.

> Duncan's personal favorite truffles are those involving fruit and herbs, like an apricot-basil version she makes in the summer months, or a pomegranate-blueberry-basil truffle.

foremost authority on all things chocolate, she still uses farm-fresh cream, local seasonal fruits, and only the most wholesome ingredients for everything she makes.

Production has expanded by leaps and bounds since her childhood days, but the sentiments remain the same. All truffles, be it a classic salted caramel or a Manhattan-flavored cocktail truffle, are hand-dipped one by one. All caramels, made from local wildflower honey and agave nectar, are dutifully stirred and infused with flavors like rosemary and sea salt. It's the quality and care that made Duncan's confections such a hit with family at Christmas, and it's the same passion that's made her an essential fixture in Chicago's sweets scene.

2745 W Armitage Ave.
773-245-1630
www.katherine-anne.com

LA SIRENA CLANDESTINA

A beachy taste of Brazil in Fulton Market

What happens when one of Chicago's most sought-after itinerant chefs puts down roots and opens his own restaurant? La Sirena Clandestina is what happens. This alluring nook on Fulton Market, which translates as "hidden mermaid" out of the notion of tropical discovery and surprise, is the handiwork of chef John Manion, a longtime fan favorite amidst Chicago's culinary scene and a unique tour de force in the kitchen.

Throughout his dynamic career, from chef positions at Goose Island and Branch 27 to revolutionary Latin restaurant Mas, Manion has always tapped into his Brazilian roots and infused his menus with South American flair. La Sirena Clandestina is the culmination of all those efforts. Although born in Detroit, Manion and his family moved to São Paulo, Brazil, when he was eight. It's this experience that filled him with culinary inspiration at such a young age, leaving him forever stimulated by the culture and cuisine of Brazil. Coupled with extensive travels through South America, La Sirena is a lush homage to his upbringing and the diverse career that followed.

Aside from a brief segue into the world of political science at Marquette University and public relations while working in D.C., the siren song of the kitchen was too strong for Manion to resist.

In 2016, Manion and company journeyed even farther by opening another restaurant in the West Loop. El Che Bar is a sultry Argentine restaurant with heavy focus on a fiery hearth stove. Items include charred quail with polenta and braised mustard greens, bone-in salmon steaks with dill salsa verde, and head-on prawns with grilled rapini and coal-roasted mojo de ajo.

Left: The main merman behind the magic, John Manion brings unique inspiration to La Sirena Clandestina.

Center: Whether seated at a table or perched at the action-packed bar, this Fulton Market hot spot is a real gem.

Right: One of the crown jewels of the menu, feijoada is a hearty medley of pork belly, grilled short ribs, linguiça sausage, black beans, rice, farofa, collard greens, and malagueta salsa. Credit Nicole Manion

He came to Chicago for culinary school and stuck around to fill up his impressive resume cooking at places like Grappa and Churrascos. His much-anticipated restaurant made a splash in 2012, capping off an illustrious professional journey and bringing everything full circle back to his earliest forays into food. His longtime fondness for the food of Brazil, Argentina, and the Caribbean manifests in a charismatic menu that isn't shy about coloring outside the lines. At La Sirena, Manion pairs salt cod fritters with cilantro remoulade and serves grilled chicken hearts with fried plantains and mojo verde, he fuses Latin flavors with a Chicago classic for his Brazilian beef sandwich loaded with roasted tri-tip and spiced beef jus, and he even gives banana cinnamon rolls a beachy finish with rum-pineapple glaze.

To dine here feels like embarking on a journey of discovery, something the well-traveled and inspired chef is well equipped to guide you through.

945 W Fulton Market
312-226-5300
www.lasirenachicago.com

LAWRY'S THE PRIME RIB

Meaty pomp and circumstance at its finest, served in a historic downtown mansion

As far as Chicago steakhouses go—and there are many—Lawry's The Prime Rib has the most colorful history. After all, it's not every day you get to dine at a steakhouse located in an allegedly haunted mansion that once contained a puppet theatre.

Opened in 1974 and still owned by the Frank family, Lawry's is located inside the historic McCormick Mansion built in 1890 just off the Magnificent Mile, which makes for quite an opulent and memorable dining experience in and of itself. The space has the look and feel of a museum more so than your standard restaurant, and it's still got the classic pomp and circumstance you'd expect from such a timeless institution.

The main dining area is the ballroom, complete with soaring ceiling, glistening chandeliers, and lavish artwork. Just on the other side of that ceiling are untouched rooms filled with puppets and old furnishings from the McCormick family, but you'd never expect such eeriness considering how elegant, refined, and non-scary things seem to be in the restaurant downstairs.

A recent innovation at Lawry's The Prime Rib is their tableside meat and potato martini, a nod to the Midwestern meat and potatoes lore. The first cocktail to be prepared and poured at the table, the drink is the handiwork of beverage director Trevor Bierwirth, who accents Chopin potato vodka with two olives stuffed with horseradish and prime rib.

Top Left: A classic steakhouse calls for a classic martini.

Above Left: Freshly carved prime rib, mashed potatoes, and warm Yorkshire pudding are the stars of the show at this show-stopping steakhouse.

Above Right: The illustrious main dining room, housed in the mansion's ballroom, is a fitting setting in which to enjoy a lavish meal.

The food is as classic as the space, with strong martinis, lobster, Yorkshire pudding, and of course that namesake prime rib—corn-fed Midwestern beef that's hand carved to order and glorious in its sublime succulence and tenderness. Dining at Lawry's is a true throwback, but fortunately not enough of a throwback to scare you before you finish your steak.

100 E Ontario St.
312-787-5000
www.lawrysonline.com/lawrys-primerib/chicago

LONGMAN & EAGLE

Tavern-inspired restaurant, bar, and inn that helped kick-start Logan Square into culinary high gear

Logan Square, one of the hottest neighborhoods in Chicago for restaurants and bars, can be divided into two eras: pre-Longman & Eagle and post-Longman & Eagle. The hyper-popular tavern/restaurant/inn was the domino that ignited a sea change on Chicago's Northwest side, beckoning a new cultural age that saw a never-ending surge of business openings throughout the area. But how does one restaurant prove so pivotal in the trajectory of a neighborhood? How does a place become the quintessential neighborhood restaurant in the quintessential neighborhood?

A lot of that has to do with the restaurant's adherence to Chicago lore and its roots as an inn. The vision of Cody Hudson, Robert McAdams, and Peter Creig Toalson of Land and Sea Dept. and Bruce Finkelman and chef Jared Wentworth of 16" On Center, Longman & Eagle is the handiwork of a dream team of hospitality vets who saw a common goal to pay homage to Chicago's inns of yore. Not only is this modern bed and breakfast format non-existent elsewhere in Logan Square, but it harkens to Chicago's oldest drinking history, to a time when most liquor was consumed at taverns with rooms onsite. Directly inspired by defunct institutions like The Eagle and The Sauganash, Longman & Eagle brought those traditions into the modern age. By bringing inn pastimes to the forefront and setting itself miles apart from other establishments in the area, Longman & Eagle feels more like a lively hipster bar than a fine-dining restaurant, the kind of antiquated saloon you might expect to find in the Wild West, with rooms upstairs in case you get sloshed on whiskey.

The front room features a large bar as its focal point, adjacent to a tiny open kitchen, while the smaller back room feels less raucous. There are six hotel rooms upstairs, each distinctly and artfully designed like an urban hostel and outfitted with funky accoutrements like cassette players and Apple TV. Considering the casual vibe and emphasis on the beverage program, the food here is

Top Left: One prime example of how Longman & Eagle thinks outside the box is fried chicken roulade, re-examining the form of a classic comfort food. Credit Clayton Hauck

Above Left: When the restaurant opened, it put a modern spin on nose-to-tail cooking, getting crafty with everything from pig face to veal brain. Credit Clayton Hauck

Above Right: It's a contemporary take on the classic American tavern, complete with lots of booze and an inn upstairs. Credit Clayton Hauck

far better than it needs to be, incorporating a bevy of seasonal and local ingredients, animal organ dishes, and even some modernist techniques, like yogurt "leather" with granola and aerated blue cheese with Buffalo frogs' legs. Dishes tend to be heavier and heartier, like wild boar sloppy joes, foie gras "whoopie pies," bone marrow, and Chicago-style pig head sandwiches. But don't ignore the lighter options either: slow-roasted cauliflower, housemade ricotta gnudi, and foraged mushroom salad are all as stellar as the meatier selections.

Equally as prominent is the bar's whiskey list. This is, at its core, a whiskey bar after all, due not only to its extensive beverage selection, but also to its dark, alluring color scheme. Their whiskey and bourbon list is huge, enabling drinkers to partake of a variety of whiskey flights and shots. There's also a deep craft beer list, a relatively shallow wine list, and a number of affordable cocktails that change with the seasons.

2657 N Kedzie Ave.
773-276-7110
www.longmanandeagle.com

LOU MITCHELL'S

Heaping portions of comfort food at Chicago's quintessential diner

After almost one hundred years in business, Chicago's most iconic diner still brings people together in a way unlike any other restaurant. On any given morning at Lou Mitchell's diner, you can still expect the same line of hungry customers, the same surly-but-doting waitresses, the same complimentary doughnut holes, and the same saucer-sized omelettes. Situated at the beginning of the famous Route 66, aka the "Mother Road" of America connecting the Midwest to the West, Lou Mitchell's has long been ideally situated to serve as a central gathering place for people from all walks of life, a sentiment this family-run institution has always taken to heart.

The frenzied diner dates back to 1923, when William Mitchell (the restaurant is named after his son, Lou) and his kin began slinging Belgian malted waffles, corned beef hash, thick-cut French toast, and their famous jumbo omelettes stuffed with the likes of Greek sausage, zucchini, and even apples and cheese. It quickly caught on not only for its convenient central location, but for its indulgent and reliable comfort food.

When Lou himself assumed ownership of the restaurant in the 1950s, things got a little quirkier, with the addition of free Milk Duds, something that helped solidify Lou Mitchell's as a diner with character. Women and children get a free fun-sized box of candy when they arrive, inspired by the Greek tradition of offering something sweet to guests. Men shouldn't feel too left out, though. Everyone still receives a free doughnut hole as they're waiting for their table.

To this day, the operation remains in the family, since Lou sold the restaurant to his niece Katherine Thanas. Unlike almost anything else in a metropolitan setting, it's still the kind of place that immediately whisks you away to another era, making you forget all about trivial day-to-day happenings, like what year it is and whether or not double-yolk eggs are good for you. The original neon sign

Very little has changed at this iconic West Loop diner over the decades. They do accept credit cards now, though.

boasting "the world's best coffee" is still in place; the squishy booths with wood tables are as comfy today as they were decades ago; and politicians still make frequent campaign stops to schmooze with regulars. Thanks in part to its location, but mostly due to its time-tested hospitality, quirks, and comforts, Lou Mitchell's has always been and always will be a place where locals and travelers alike can sit side by side and share in a common experience that connects us all.

565 W Jackson Blvd.
312-939-3111
www.loumitchellsrestaurant.com

LULA CAFE

The birthplace of the farm-to-table movement

Long before Logan Square was the scene-y hot spot it is today, there was Lula Cafe. For years, the charming contemporary American restaurant has been a staple in the area, truly defining what it means to be not only a neighborhood haunt, but a pioneer in the farm-to-table evolution.

Fast-forward to today, as Logan Square balloons with trendy restaurants and bars, and Lula remains the much-adored standard it's always been, aging with as much grace as Meryl Streep. Lula is run by husband-wife team Jason Hammel and Amalea Tshilds, who anticipated the Logan Square gentrification boom when they opened their restaurant in 1999, and like the neighborhood, Lula has evolved over the years and only gotten better. What started off as a casual breakfast spot has morphed into one of the best brunch spots in the city, supplemented by a high-end dinner menu and a solid bar program.

It's the rare restaurant that successfully caters to a wide swath of clientele. Diners can come here for a quick sandwich, a leisurely brunch, a date night, a high-end dinner, or anything in between. The restaurant features two distinct menus: the cafe menu which offers casual dishes like sandwiches, quesadillas, and surprisingly revelatory spaghetti, and the dinner menu which skews towards composed entrees, seasonal ingredients, and meticulous presentations. The cafe menu is augmented with brunch specials during the day, and the core offerings are available all day and night, so no matter what time you come, you can adjust your meal to your budget and liking.

Locally sourced food is the focus at Lula, and Hammel impresses with his creative flavor combinations. The chef/owner dubs his style "naturalism," which he describes as plating vegetables as they appear in nature. So now you'll understand why the romaine leaves on the Caesar salad are uncut, which make for a crisp, albeit ungraceful bite. It's something he's been passionate about his whole life, since spending time in his grandparents' restaurant in Connecticut. Lula's bar sports a decent beer selection, plus cocktails and wines. Make sure you save room for great seasonal desserts, and in the a.m., be

Left: While the main menus change almost daily per seasonal, local ingredients, Lula also sports a regular cafe menu with casual mainstays like spaghetti. Photo by Kyle Kissel

Center: Brunch was fashionable at Lula Cafe long before the weekend meal became all the rage. Photo by Kyle Kissel

Right: Jason Hammel helped pioneer the farm-to-table movement in Chicago. The chef has been cooking with seasonal, fresh ingredients for years. Photo by Kyle Kissel

sure to sample the pastries, such as smoked pecan sticky buns and Meyer lemon pound cake.

An addition/renovation has added quite a bit of space to the restaurant, including a snazzy new front bar, a number of extra (and necessary) tables, and a new pastry kitchen. The entry room and bar area adjoin the second dining room through a small hallway. Here, the restaurant feels more upscale, complete with a long marble bar and a peek into the kitchen. Despite the revamp, Lula is as charming as ever, always maintaining that humility and wholesomeness that made it the neighborhood keystone in the first place.

2537 N Kedzie Ave.
773-489-9554
www.lulacafe.com

MANNY'S CAFETERIA & DELICATESSEN

Chicago's go-to for corned beef sandwiches, potato pancakes, matzo ball soup, and other olden deli classics

Every major city has its legendary old-school delicatessen. In New York City, it's Katz's Delicatessen. Los Angeles has Canter's Deli. Here in Chicago, that title belongs to Manny's Deli & Cafeteria in the South Loop. In its current location since 1964, Manny's is the type of seasoned institution with just as much character as corned beef, where endearingly gruff staffers fill up cafeteria trays with matzo ball soup and Reuben sandwiches with ninja-like rigor. Since its inception, Manny's has remained a family-run business, currently owned by the late Manny Raskin's son Ken, who runs the busy restaurant with his wife Patti and their kids Danny, Jason, Stephanie, and Matt. It's as family-oriented as it's always been, since Jack Raskin named his Jewish deli after his son Emanuel, aka Manny. The namesake also served as a cook, honing the classic recipes that still attract hungry customers, both regulars and tourists, today. This includes hulking sandwiches with cult followings, like corned beef, pastrami, and beef brisket with so much meat that the bread gets buried. Mac and cheese, potato pancakes, knishes, sweet potato pie, Salisbury steak, meatloaf, and rice pudding are a few more highlights on the sprawling menu. For decades, Manny's has always been about hospitality and family-inspired recipes, sentiments that have helped the restaurant become the crowd-pleasing legend it is today.

1141 S Jefferson St.
312-939-2855
www.mannysdeli.com

Top: Heaping plates of corned beef wouldn't be complete without a side of freshly fried potato pancakes.

Bottom Left: In addition to popular mainstays like pastrami and matzo ball soup, Manny's rotates hearty specials throughout the week.

Bottom Right: Chicago's most iconic delicatessen and cafeteria has been in its current location since 1964.

Manny's expanded its Chicago footprint in 2002 when it opened a spinoff location at Midway Airport.

Timeless contemporary cuisine from one of Chicago's finest

When it comes to legacy-making restaurants in Chicago (and the country at large), mk The Restaurant has had more impact than just about any place in the city. The same can be said of its chef-owner, Michael Kornick. Right up there with local legends like the bygone Charlie Trotter's and Trio, mk has molded a stunning amount of talent and helped catapult careers for chefs in Chicago and beyond.

Mindy Segal of HotChocolate fame; Dave Beran, formerly of Fulton Market's innovative Next; Tony Galzin of Nashville's Nicky's Coal Fired; and Bradley Rubin of Eleven City Diner are just a few of the names who have passed through mk's venerable doors over the years. Its subsequent successes are a testament to Kornick's leadership and passion, something imbued in him early on by his family.

He started cooking at a young age with his grandmother and mother, and he knew he wanted to be a chef by age eleven. His interests only grew from there, and by eighteen, he was captivated by the craftsmanship of food and the energy of restaurants. His father, meanwhile, always encouraged him to follow his passion and pursue it relentlessly. And so he did, going on to work under esteemed chefs like Gordon Sinclair of Gordon Restaurant and Barry Wine at New York's The Quilted Giraffe.

In 2009, Kornick partnered with David Morton to form DMK Restaurants, a branch that operates some of Chicago's best casual chef-driven destinations. These include various locations of DMK Burger Bar, plus Fish Bar, Ada Street, County Barbecue, and Henry's.

mk doesn't need many bells and whistles to delight and comfort its guests. The restaurant remains as timelessly elegant and tasteful as ever.

By the time he was twenty-eight, Kornick was hired as executive chef of the Four Seasons Hotel Boston, before moving back to Chicago to help open critically lauded Marche and Red Light. Then came the opportunity to open his own restaurant, which he did with his wife Lisa in 1998, on an off-the-beaten stretch of River North.

Year after year, mk proves its staying power with a staunch commitment to classical cooking techniques, seasonal ingredients, and its continued position as a breeding ground of talent. Nowadays, the executive chef is Erick Williams, a man who started on the salad station when the restaurant first opened, gradually moving up the ranks over the years. Under Kornick, Williams, and pastry chef Lisa Bonjour, the restaurant has aged with remarkable grace, retaining just the right amount of understated elegance and a refreshingly straightforward menu of contemporary American fare.

The menu and the space are both essentially blank canvasses that leave guests wondering what's to emerge from the kitchen, and while dishes may sound straightforward on paper (baby Spanish octopus grilled over hardwood charcoal, cumin-scented parsnip bisque, and roasted Peking duck breast with blueberry and cocoa reduction are a few recent highlights), even a restaurant as enduring as this one is still serving up surprises that can teach the new restaurants in town a thing or two.

868 N Franklin St.
312-482-9179
www.mkchicago.com

"My core beliefs are that the best restaurants are places that focus on the guests' needs, wants, and desires," explains Kornick. "They don't have great egos. Great restaurants cater to their guests with devotion and empathy. They serve their community and contribute to the industry by providing mentorship to new people entering the industry. They respect and care for the shared environment. They work to promote sustainable, safe, and healthy food sources. They respect the earth. At mk, at our core we are a mom-and-pop restaurant that exists because of our great people. Our mk team works extremely hard every day to be a better restaurant for the community we serve."

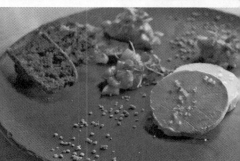

Above Left: Soaring, lofty ceilings afford plenty of opportunities for unique art installations.

Top Right: Some of the finest and freshest fish in town can be found at mk.

Above Right: Foie gras is a classic appetizer at this classic Chicago restaurant.

MOODY TONGUE TAPROOM

Culinary beers as tasty as the German chocolate cake

When a trained chef turns his talents towards beer, magical things happen. Aptly dubbed "culinary brewing," it's an increasingly popular trend in the craft beer scene made famous by places like Moody Tongue Brewery, and it's all courtesy of the multitalented brewmaster, Jared Rouben.

A graduate of the prestigious Culinary Institute of America in New York, Rouben initially embarked on a culinary career, clocking time at Napa's famed Martini House and even Thomas Keller's Per Se in New York City. With a kitchen career off to such a promising start, the burgeoning talent opted to pivot from food to beer as a means of pursuing a longtime hobby. While in cooking school, Rouben founded the Brew Club. As he cooked, he began to recognize similarities between cooking and brewing that made him want to take his education and experiences in an unexplored direction. "Culinary brewing" began to take shape as a means of infusing offbeat ingredients into beers during the brewing process, ingredients more commonly seen on plates than in glassware.

From persimmons to black truffles, Rouben took his ideas to higher and higher levels in Chicago, where he attended the Siebel Institute and served as a boundary-pushing brewmaster for Goose Island Brewpubs, routinely perusing farmers' markets for fresh

In addition to a steady lineup of crowd-pleasing beers, Moody Tongue regularly rotates limited-availability beers and seasonal creations. These include a Bourbon Barrel Aged Chocolate Barleywine, a Shaved Black Truffle Pilsner, and a Gingerbread Imperial Stout.

Top Left: Hard not to love a place where towering slices of German chocolate cake are one of only two food items on the menu.

Above Left: On the savory side, freshly shucked oysters pair nicely with many of Moody Tongue's culinary brews.

Above Right: The Moody Tongue Taproom is far from your average beer bar.

inspiration and provisions. He quickly developed a reputation for his experimental brews, and he was eventually inspired to branch out and create a culinary brewery all his own. Moody Tongue is a Pilsen brewery and taproom that serves as a showcase for beers like his Sliced Nectarine IPA and the dessert-in-a-glass Caramelized Chocolate Churro Baltic Porter. As if these novel potables weren't original enough, the taproom is something unique in and of itself.

With a fireplace, bookshelves, and gorgeous lounge chairs, the space feels more like a Victorian parlor than a beer bar. To eat, Rouben has curated a concise menu consisting of only two things: German chocolate cake and raw oysters. According to the brewmaster, these represent the ideal sweet and savory counterpoints to his beers.

2136 S Peoria St.
312-600-5111
www.moodytongue.com/the-tasting-room

DOUGHNUT VAULT Word of caution to claustrophobes: Doughnut Vault is teeny tiny.

312 CHICAGO From bracing Negronis to an ample Italian wine list, the beverage program's got something for everyone. *Photo by Jason Little*

AU CHEVAL You should line up now if you want a chance to try Au Cheval's almighty burger. *Photo by Kevin Miyazaki*

BIG JONES Even something as simple as banana pudding gets an authentic makeover.

NAHA Pastry chef Craig Harzewski is on dessert duty, constantly dazzling with gorgeous presentations and thoughtful combinations of flavors and textures.

Photo by Ryan Beshel

BOLEO One of the more distinctive desserts in the Loop, cherimoya mousse employs a creamy South American fruit as a base, along with yogurt sponge cake, pineapple pearls, and white chocolate powder. *Photo by David Szymanski*

NORTH POND From seafood to market-fresh produce, Bruce Sherman has a knack for combining uncommon flavor pairings with incredible results.

FAT RICE BAKERY The Bakery at Fat Rice, located right next door to the restaurant, features quirky Asian and Portuguese pastries like these pork-filled "honey pigs." *Photo courtesy of Fat Rice Bakery*

SPINNING J Dinah Grossman is the pastry pro behind Spinning J's incomparable sweets. *Photo by Clayton Hauck*

ACADIA Every dish is prepared and presented with surgical precision at Acadia.

LONGMAN & EAGLE One prime example of how Longman & Eagle thinks outside the box is fried chicken roulade, re-examining the form of a classic comfort food. *Photo credit Clayton Hauck*

HONEY BUTTER FRIED CHICKEN "The OG" sandwich features fried chicken strips, candied jalapeño mayo, and crunchy slaw on a buttery bun.
Photo credit Tim Musho

SOUTHPORT GROCERY & CAFE Smoked brisket, ham, Gruyère, Dijonnaise, giardiniera, and arugula, all heaped on grilled housemade bread, fill up the cafe's Cuban sandwich.

HOTCHOCOLATE Obviously, any of the restaurant's rich-as-fudge namesake hot chocolates are not to miss. *Photo by Anthony Tahlier*

GIRL & THE GOAT A standout dish on the menu since day one, wood-oven roasted pig face comes with a sunny-side egg, tamarind, cilantro, red wine-maple, and crunchy potato "stix." *Photo by Anthony Tahlier*

R. J. GRUNTS Sitting at one of R. J. Grunts's storied booths is like traveling back in time.

You haven't tasted cupcakes like these before

Less isn't always more. Sometimes more is more. That's true at least when it comes to elevating the cupcake to an art form at the Gold Coast's aptly dubbed cupcake boutique, more (the shop's name is all lower-case. Less a cupcake shop and more (pun intended) an art gallery-meets-bakery, this gorgeous little nook features some of the prettiest and most inventive desserts in Chicago.

By using the cupcake as a base form for flavor innovation, they've adapted unique combinations in all kinds of inventive ways, some of which skew savory and others boozy. More first emerged in September 2008 from visionary and self-proclaimed cupcake curator Patty Rothman. Her idea was simple: to take something everyone loved when they were younger and evolve it—to make it more. She does so in all kinds of nifty ways, by mixing and matching American and Italian buttercreams, by glazing cakes with delicate ganaches, by garnishing with addictive brittles, and by pushing the envelope with out-of-the-box flavors like white truffle and even a BLT cupcake made with a bacon-studded cake, ranch buttercream, micro lettuce garnishes, and slivered cherry tomatoes.

When the shop first opened, it was during a time when everyone was doing bold flavors and capturing attention with audacious dishes. Rothman and company jumped on board with their roster of fun, outlandish flavors, many of which were directly inspired by dishes she'd try at restaurants or cocktails she'd sip, all with the notion of "this flavor profile would make a great cupcake!" Since those days, they've whittled their portfolio down to what customers really love and crave the most. All the while, everything is still made from scratch on a daily basis, never frozen, and always from the utmost ingredients, even if those ingredients are top-shelf Champagnes or pricey rare truffles. Rest assured, patrons can still find those more exotic savory flavors at Chicago's most inventive

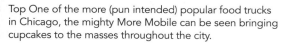

Top One of the more (pun intended) popular food trucks in Chicago, the mighty More Mobile can be seen bringing cupcakes to the masses throughout the city.

Center: The namesake more cupcake is an homage to a Hostess classic, complete with cream filling, rich chocolate, and a drizzle of icing on top.

Bottom: Booze-infused cocktail cupcakes are a fun option here, available in flavors like margarita, lemon drop, and bourbon chocolate bourbon. Cheers to that.

The namesake signature cupcake is Rothman's ode to the iconic Hostess cupcake with the drizzled icing logo. Here, the more cupcake is a dark Valrhona chocolate cake filled with cream, glazed with chocolate ganache, and drizzled with the word "more."

cupcake shop, like strawberry-black pepper-balsamic and mango-cilantro, along with booze-infused varieties like bourbon-chocolate and chocolate-Champagne, but the crux of more's arsenal is reserved for iconic sweets like salted caramel, cookies and cream, and a particularly striking lemon meringue cupcake. According to Rothman, these are flavors that personify the idea of "doing more" with something classic, all while fitting neatly into the idea of comfort food raised to an art.

1 E. Delaware Pl.
312-951-0001
www.morecupcakes.com

NAHA

Midwestern ingredients meet Mediterranean inspirations

NAHA has been a pillar in River North for well over a decade, and it still manages to stay fresh and exciting thanks to the tireless talents of executive chef Carrie Nahabedian and her deft culinary team. As with many good chefs, Nahabedian cites both her mother and Julia Child as chief influences in developing an interest in cooking, so much so that she enrolled in an apprenticeship program with the Ritz-Carlton in Chicago.

The rest of Nahabedian's colorful career took her all over the world, from hotel to hotel and restaurant to restaurant. But despite clocking time working at restaurants as far-flung as California and Europe, she always came back to her hometown. She came back to work at Le Perroquet. She came back to work at Le Francais. And ultimately, she came back again to open her own restaurant. Along with her cousin Michael Nahabedian, who helms the beverage side, and several other family members, Nahabedian put her well-traveled experiences and inspirations to good use with a restaurant uniquely focused on seasonal American cuisine with Middle Eastern and Armenian influences.

Syrian pumpkin seed oil, Armenian lahmajoon lamb pizza, and feta cheese boereg are a few examples of items you can expect to find speckled throughout the menus, right alongside lacquered duck breast, honey-roasted red kuri squash, and New Zealand venison, to name just a few. Plates are lavish and complex, brimming with ingredients rigorously sourced both from local farms (anything Nahabedian does with maple syrup from Indiana's Maplewood Farms is a must-order) and faraway destinations, like oysters from Vancouver. The chef also favors sweet and savory combinations, like her omnipresent foie gras dish, which rotates accompaniments but always includes a sweet note, such as a fruit tarte Tatin or a marmalade. You'd be remiss to skip dessert.

Under the direction of seasoned pastry chef Craig Harzewski, who also bakes all the breads for the restaurant (and quirky mignardises

Top: Elegant preparations of foie gras are par for the course at one of River North's most revered restaurants. Photo by Ryan Beshel

Center: Pastry chef Craig Harzewski is a veritable wizard when it comes to artfully presented desserts. Photo by Ryan Beshel

Bottom: NAHA is always one of the best restaurants to check out for stunning interpretations of seasonal, local ingredients, like fiddlehead ferns in the spring. Photo by Ryan Beshel

September 22, 2009, was a big day for Carrie Nahabedian. In addition to being dedicated as Carrie Nahabedian Day by former mayor Richard M. Daley, it's the date she was inducted into the Chicago Culinary Museum Chefs Hall of Fame.

like housemade Peeps around Easter time), desserts sway from opulent—gâteau Basque custard cake with olive oil ice cream, Bartlett pears, soft polenta, and pomegranate—to whimsical—sundaes with caramel, hazelnuts, dark chocolate, porter beer ice cream, and an adjoining "Nutella" panini.

The restaurant itself is sleek and contemporary, an impressive achievement for a business at this venerable stage in its existence. A place this mature and longstanding should be showing some age, but NAHA is somehow sleek and lustrous, even youthful. It remains one of the preeminent restaurants in Chicago, and when it's not too busy, it can be one of the most romantic, so don't be surprised if a couple gets engaged next to you.

500 N Clark St.
312-321-6242
www.naha-chicago.com

Feel like part of the family at this Latin-flavored Bridgeport staple

With a name like Nana, it's no wonder that family is at the core of Bridgeport's homiest restaurant. It gets its name from Maria "Nana" Solis, the mother of owners Omar and Christian Solis, and she's still a regular fixture at the restaurant, making the rounds throughout the dining room to greet guests in the very same building where she raised her family upstairs.

While the space previously housed a bar, the Solis brothers leapt at the opportunity to turn it into a family restaurant when it became available, both to give Bridgeport a wholesome and reliable dining destination and to create a business hinged on family. Nana the restaurant became a manifestation of Nana the matriarch—a comforting, familiar place where customers are made to feel like cherished neighbors being welcomed into a dinner party. Or a breakfast party. Or a lunch party.

Being a family-run restaurant named after the family matriarch, it's no surprise that Nana has one of the best kids' menus in Chicago. The aim was to offer children items that are at once tasty and wholesome. Since the restaurant's namesake has grandkids herself, she's well versed in cooking for young ones. With several options to choose from throughout the day, many featuring organic ingredients as often as possible, dishes include mini French toast, grilled quesadillas, grilled peanut butter and jam sandwiches, mac and cheese, mini burgers, and more.

Left: With a menu that's largely organic and always incredibly fresh, dining at Nana is an experience you can feel good about.

Center: Tapping into its Latin roots, the restaurant features classic regional dishes like empanadas.

Right: Renowned for their brunch, you can rest assured that Nana features some decadent dessert items masquerading as breakfast.

The food—a mix of American and Latin flavors with an eye toward seasonality, local sourcing, and organic ingredients—is a direct reflection of the kind of food Nana has always liked to cook at home. This includes beef-filled empanadas, Cuban sandwiches, pan-roasted trout with chili-lime cream, and pupusas, doughy baked masa patties, popular in Latin cuisines, that are used in place of English muffins in the restaurant's signature "Nanadict" with poached eggs, chorizo, and poblano cream sauce. The desserts in particular are all the handiwork of Nana herself. Prior to opening the restaurant, she was on pastry duty at Lakeview's defunct Cafe 28; now she's keeping things sweet in Bridgeport with tres leches and rum cakes.

For the Solis family, operating their own restaurant together is the culmination of their dream, and it never feels like work when you're doing what you love with the ones you love.

3267 S Halsted St.
312-929-2486
www.nanaorganic.com

Modern American fare as memorable as the picturesque setting

One of the most entrancing restaurants in Chicago is one with a serious eye for simplicity. The innate awe of North Pond can largely be credited to its unparalleled location in the middle of Lincoln Park, on the shores of its namesake pond.

The restaurant is housed in a bygone ice skating shelter built in 1912, at the height of the Arts and Crafts architecture movement, which was popularized as a rebellion against the lavish styles of the Victorian era. Its central tenet was to let the building materials shine without extra adornment, and it's a philosophy that ties in handily with chef Bruce Sherman's cuisine; he seeks out the best in local products and prepares sublimely simple dishes with them. He also eschews mass-produced ingredients in favor of items he can get at the nearby farmers' market or from Midwestern farms.

That ethos is one he picked up while cooking and working in New Delhi, India, where daily visits to the local vegetable market dictated the day's itinerary, utilizing only what was fresh and seasonal. Back in his hometown of Chicago, the North Pond experience is much more than mere dinner, since it entails a lovely stroll through the park and around the North Pond Nature Sanctuary. The heart of Sherman's restaurant is his seasonal tasting menu (you can also dine a la carte).

Consistent with the restraint of the Arts and Crafts movement, the name of each dish simply comprises the featured ingredients, like an appetizer called "beef, seaweed," an entree named "wood pigeon, apple" and a dessert dubbed "lemon, huckleberry."

But true to form, there's a lot of artistry in simplicity, and beneath each modestly titled dish is something extraordinary. That "beef, seaweed" starter is actually beef tenderloin tartare with West Coast oyster, maple miroir, fresh Monterey seaweed, puffed rice, and pears, while "lemon, huckleberry" begets a grand finale of hot lemon ricotta soufflé with huckleberry syrup, pistachio ice cream, cake croutes, and huckleberry jellies.

Top: Like the historic architecture of the building, North Pond feels like a space preserved in time from a bygone era.

Center: The restaurant gets its name from the glistening pond on which it sits, surrounded by lush trees and grassy hills.

Bottom: One of the most beautiful restaurant settings in Chicago, North Pond requires a stroll through Lincoln Park to access it.

"I guess I'm genetically predisposed to it," says Sherman of his initial interest in cooking. "Early on, I took an interest in watching my mother prepare food at home on a daily basis. Compounded by my father's obsessive-compulsive interest in 'retail' food, like grocery stores and delis, I think it was meant to be."

Immersed in nature, in the shadows of Lincoln Park trees, there really couldn't be a more fitting setting for embracing simplicity in all its natural, organic glory and showcasing how stunning that simplicity can really be.

2610 N Cannon Dr.
773-477-5845
www.northpondrestaurant.com

Inventive, ever-changing tasting menus in a comfortable loft-like dining room

You never know when inspiration will strike. Sometimes a spicy meal in Chinatown may trigger an idea for a new dish; sometimes a trip to New Orleans might tap into a taste memory. Vivid inspirations are the pulse of Oriole, a sign-less restaurant tucked down a quiet side street in the West Loop. Guests enter through a nondescript door and through the back of an old freight elevator to access the loft-like dining room, where inspired tasting menus are the order of the day.

Course after course has a story to it, all courtesy of executive chef/owner Noah Sandoval and pastry chef/partner Genie Kwon. Both chefs have amassed considerable respect and fandom in the Chicago restaurant community in relatively short periods of time: Sandoval dazzled diners with his take on gluten-free fine dining at the defunct Senza, while Kwon cut her pastry teeth at high-end spots like Boka, GT Fish & Oyster, and The Peninsula, in addition to restaurants in Boston and New York City. Their synergy is palpable in the wide-open kitchen, as the two split the tasting menu evenly into savory and sweet, both drawing upon past experiences and memories to curate degustations rich with passion.

Although menus change frequently, one plate might feature a three-day confit lamb belly inspired by Sandoval's favorite dish at Chinatown's Lao Sze Chuan, swapping the proteins and outfitting the dish with Chinese-inspired additions like Sichuan chili, coriander, and anise hyssop.

On the dessert side, Kwon might transport diners to her hometown of New Orleans, a city where Sandoval and his wife Cara both lived as well. Before they opened Oriole together, they all went on a trip to the Big Easy to bond and find inspiration. One thing that came of the trip, after an essential visit to the French Quarter's famed Café Du Monde, was a dessert of milk ice cream, Tahitian vanilla-cinnamon crumble, and whiskey-orange foam.

Top: The food may be elaborate and meticulous, but the loft-like space keeps things comfortable and relaxed.

Bottom: Another caviar iteration looks like something from another planet.

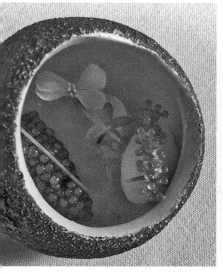

Although one of Chicago's newer fine-dining restaurants, opened in 2016, Oriole quickly caught on with both critics and the dining public. It earned an impressive two stars from Michelin in its first year and a four-star review from the Chicago Tribune, among many other accolades.

For Sandoval and Kwon, inspiration comes in many forms, manifesting in different dishes and techniques on a constant basis. For patrons, a meal at this comfortable fine-dining destination means embarking on a journey of taste memories that help build new memories entirely.

661 W Walnut St.
312-877-5339
www.oriolechicago.com

The deep-dish tradition gets a caramelized twist

When people think of Chicago-style pizza, the form is often monopolized by heavy-hitting downtown institutions like Pizzeria Uno, Giordano's, Lou Malnati's, and Gino's East. That's all well and good, but if you want quintessential Chicago-style deep-dish done right, you have to head to Pequod's. Like any good deep-dish spot, this one comes with a bit of history, showing just how convoluted and interwoven the local pizza community really is.

The original concept dates back to 1970 in Morton Grove, where Pequod's developed a quiet cult following for its deep-dish pizzas served on caramelized crusts. This was a technique where pizza-makers would line the exterior of the dough with a sprinkling of cheese; that way, when it baked it would caramelize and develop more crispiness and flavor. The original location was the handiwork of pizza legend Burt Katz, who would go on to open his own famous pizzeria called Burt's Place before shuttering it in 2015 and passing away in 2016.

After Katz sold Pequod's in 1986 to Keith Jackson, the menu expanded and popularity grew. Then in 1992, Jackson brought Pequod's into the city with a Lincoln Park location, immediately positioning itself as one of the best pizzerias in a city renowned for its pizza. This unassuming, cavernous tavern serves some of the best pizza in Chicago, thanks to a well-honed formula that elevates the deep-dish form to new heights. The key, to this day, is in that caramelized crust. It might look a bit burnt around the edges, but that's all crunch, and it's a welcome contrast to the ooey-gooey pizza innards. Like most Chicago-style pizzas, they take about thirty minutes to bake, so be prepared to wait.

2207 N Clybourn Ave.
773-327-1512
www.pequodspizza.com

Top: Decorated with an abundance of sports paraphernalia and outfitted like an American tavern, Pequod's feels like a love letter to Chicago.

Center: Don't be fooled, this is knife-and-fork pizza.

Bottom: The caramelized crust is key in setting Pequod's apart from the deep-dish herd.

Burt Katz was quite the literary devotee. Prior to opening Pequod's, which he named after the boat in *Moby Dick*, he opened another pizzeria in Chicago's Rogers Park neighborhood called Gulliver's, so named for *Gulliver's Travels*. Today, the Pequod's logo is a whale.

PICCOLO SOGNO

Pastas, pizzas, antipasti, and patio, all present and absolutely perfect

Piccolo Sogno translates to "little dream" in Italian, a fitting title considering it's one of the most quixotic Italian restaurants in Chicago. It's also a dream come true for chef/owner Tony Priolo, who first started cooking alongside his Sicilian grandmother while growing up in Chicago. Not only did she teach him the logistics of cooking and shopping for ingredients, but she also imparted to him the more important tenet that the best food comes from the heart.

It's a sentiment Priolo carried with him, from his first job as a prep cook at a local Italian restaurant to the Cooking and Hospitality Institute of Chicago and to Coco Pazzo Cafe, where he served as opening executive chef in 1997. Along with Coco Pazzo, which he helped open the following year, Priolo was quickly developing local renown for his Italian cooking.

Years later, in 2008, the chef and his business partner Ciro Longobardo realized their dream of opening their own restaurant. With Piccolo Sogno, Priolo has the opportunity to cook from the heart, like his grandmother taught him and like he's always strived to do. His philosophy is simple: source the best ingredients, prepare them simply, and let the quality speak for itself. The result is a menu brimming with some of the finest Italian food this side of the Adriatic. Start with any of the fresh insalatas or antipasti, such as cecina fritta (chickpea flour fries), ribolitta (bread soup), or the

In 2016, Priolo and Longobardo branched out with Nonnina in River North. The restaurant, named after and inspired by Italian grandmothers, features comforting portions of meatballs, sausage and peppers, bucatini carbonara, chicken Vesuvio, and lots more.

Left: One of the menu standouts is the spaghetti neri, string-cut pasta swirled with clams, mussels, shrimp, and calamari.

Center: Comfortable and relaxed, the Piccolo Sogno dining rooms provide the perfect setting in which to gather with friends, family, and Italian food.

Right: Freshly shaved truffles add a nice lavish touch to any of the restaurant's fresh pastas.

more standard fried calamari. Pastas and pizzas are composed with a refined hand, allowing the fresh ingredients to shine. Try the "straw and hay" (green and white noodles in veal ragu), the frutti di mare lush with pristine seafood, or a prosciutto pizza, cooked in a wood-fired oven and draped with razor-thin ribbons of that buttery Italian ham that dissolves in your mouth like porcine cotton candy.

The feasting doesn't stop there. Priolo is like a doting Italian grandmother, offering more and more and more Italian comfort food, like his slow-stewed rabbit with semolina pudding and his roasted duck with fennel sausage and farro polenta. This is rustic Italian cuisine at its finest. Be sure to wind down with a few scoops of housemade gelato.

The impressive and all-Italian wine list, curated by Longobardo, is a veritable bible of vino. With numerous wines by the glass, and page upon page of red and white wines categorized by their respective Italian regions (including about thirty Barolos), there is something for everybody. The restaurant is also home to one of most adored outdoor patios in Chicago. Unlike anything you'd expect to see in a bustling urban setting, the secluded space is surrounded by trees and tall wooden fencing, creating a cozy atmosphere that feels worlds away from city life. Everything about this place, from the pastoral patio to the heartwarming pastas, is indeed as dreamy as they come.

464 N Halsted St.
312-421-0077
www.piccolosognorestaurant.com

PLEASANT HOUSE BAKERY

Pastoral British inspirations beget meat pies, trifles, and garden-fresh ingredients

For many people, multitasking can be a challenge. But the folks behind Pleasant House Bakery make it look like a piece of cake. Part bread bakery, part pub, part wholesale operator, and part urban farm, they're all seamless parts of a larger puzzle that pays homage to a simpler time, when food came fresh from gardens and bread baking was a prominent pastime.

The dexterous pair behind the brand? Art and Chelsea Jackson, a dynamic duo who have grown Pleasant House into one of the most visible and successful small businesses in Chicago, with a veritable homey empire under their belts. The couple named their company after the Pleasant House cottage near Yorkshire, England, where previous Jackson generations lived in the mid-1900s.

The setting is an Eden of fresh, pastoral food that lends inspiration to the cooking and baking at their full-service restaurant and bar, Pleasant House Pub in Pilsen. This includes curry chips, Scotch eggs, buttered peas, and their signature Royal Pies, savory pot pie–like creations filled with the likes of steak, chicken balti, and mushrooms and kale.

Pleasant House has a nice symbiotic relationship with The Plant, a net-zero-energy facility in the Back of the Yards neighborhood. This is where Pleasant House Bread does all its baking and where Pleasant Farms does most of its growing. The Jacksons also employ other businesses at The Plant for use at the Pub, including coffee from 4 Letter Word Coffee and beer from Whiner Beer Co.

Top Left: Known as "Royal Pies," these pot pie-like creations are a signature favorite at Pleasant House, filled with ingredients like steak, mushrooms, and kale. Credit Dan Goldberg

Above Left: The husband-wife duo behind the Pleasant House brand: Art and Chelsea Jackson. Credit John Towner

Above Right: Coffee, pastries, beer, savory pies, and other British-inspired delicacies can be found at Pleasant House Pub. Credit Dan Goldberg

Art mans the savory side, while Chelsea's pastry skills produce sticky toffee pudding and seasonal fruit trifles layered with sponge cake, custard, and whipped cream. The family cottage also inspired their wood-fired hearth breads, sold by the loaf in varieties like ciabatta, whole-wheat sourdough, and rugbrød, a heady Danish-style rye. Then there's Pleasant Farms, a small collection of urban farms scattered around Chicago's South Side and suburbs.

The Jacksons grow produce and herbs for use in their kitchen and for sale at area farmers' markets. In more ways than one, the Jacksons planted the seeds of change when they started their company as a farm in 2010, and it's since blossomed into a fruitful success story of heritage and wholesome cooking.

2119 S Halsted St.
773-523-7437
www.pleasanthousebakery.com

The birthplace of the salad bar and a restaurant empire

For Chicago-based Lettuce Entertain You Enterprises, one of the biggest and most successful restaurant groups in the country, it all started with R. J. Grunts. Open since 1971 in Lincoln Park, the cozy restaurant still wafts of nostalgia and comfort, both in the sense of its timeless, funky motif and its all-American menu filled with burgers, Buffalo chicken, pot roast, milkshakes, and so much more. For a titanic restaurant group like Lettuce Entertain You, which boasts such varied establishments as fine-dining classic Tru and perpetually packed tiki bar Three Dots and a Dash, it's pretty astonishing that it all grew out of something so modest.

It's where prolific restaurateur and local legend Rich Melman first made his mark—the restaurant got its name from the initials of Rich and his first business partner, Jerry Orzoff (plus the sound a pig makes when it eats). When the two met in 1970, Melman's innovative ideas for hospitality coupled with Orzoff's support and real estate acumen to create a lively and casual restaurant for all. Between the inviting, artsy space and the something-for-everyone menu, it didn't take long for the family-friendly eatery to earn its credibility.

This is also the place credited as Chicago's first legit salad bar, a tradition that lives on today with its popular assortment of fifty-plus customizable ingredients. The lettuce-filled salad bar became such an instant hit that it even helped inspire the name of the restaurant group.

The restaurant also has a reputation for its burgers, still a personal favorite of Melman's, from the classic cheeseburger to the namesake Gruntburger made with fried onions and blue cheese. R. J. Grunts's success is what inspired Melman and Orzoff to continue opening restaurants, and although Orzoff passed away in 1981, Melman was forever inspired to pursue their shared dream.

Top Left: Comforting Americana is R. J. Grunts's strong suit. This is evident in crowd-pleasing plates like finger-licking chicken wings.

Top Right: In part responsible for the restaurant group's name, Lettuce Entertain You Enterprises, the salad bar quickly became a sensation and remains so today.

Bottom Left: Step inside the cozy confines of one of Chicago's most enduring family-friendly restaurants, where the ambience is as comforting as the food.

Bottom Right: It's everything you love about Buffalo chicken wings, in sandwich form.

2056 N Lincoln Park W.
773-929-5363
www.rjgruntschicago.com

REVIVAL FOOD HALL

Beloved restaurants from all over the city come together to form downtown's best food hall

Just as food halls reached an exhaustive fever pitch in the United States, with thematic versions popping up in cities across the country, Revival Food Hall re-inspired the form in the heart of downtown Chicago. Rather than strive for a Disney World-like motif, as befalls many a food hall, Revival simply paid homage to the city itself, bringing the best of the neighborhoods into the nexus of the Loop's Financial District.

It's genius in its simplicity, and it's been a smash hit since day one, all thanks to Bruce Finkelman and Craig Golden. The gentlemen run a hospitality group called 16" on Center, responsible for some of Chicago's most beloved crowd-pleasers, from The Promontory in Hyde Park and MONEYGUN cocktail bar in the West Loop to Punch House in Pilsen and the venerable Empty Bottle in Ukrainian Village. These guys know Chicago and its neighborhoods like the backs of their hands, making them well-suited ambassadors for bringing a taste of the city's diverse neighborhoods to the Loop.

Both raised in Chicago's north suburbs, they each worked food jobs in high school and college before meeting in the 1990s at The Lakeshore Theater comedy club. The pair became fast friends, promoting events together before joining forces to help open Logan Square's wildly popular Longman & Eagle. Their partnership grew, leading them to far corners of the city to open unique bars and restaurants in unexpected settings.

In addition to a nice online store for stylish apparel and accessories, Revival Food Hall also features an onsite shop called Curbside Books & Records, filled with music, books, and comics from local artists and authors.

Top Left: Fresh fish bowls, sandwiches and salads are staples at Brown Bag Seafood Co. Photo by Neil Burger

Above Left: Cured meats come as platters or burly sandwiches at Danke. Photo by Lenny Gilmore

Above Right: Whether you're eating healthy or indulging, Graze Kitchenette caters to both crowds with its superfood bowls and burgers. Photo by Jennifer Catherine Photography

Combining their talents, Finkelman and Golden are able to design, renovate, own, operate, and hone food menus all in-house, making 16" on Center a powerhouse hospitality group, and one with profound vision. Their penchant for bold, daring ventures and immersive concepts led them to their most ambitious undertaking to date, a sprawling twenty-four-thousand-square-foot food hall in a historic Loop building that they've conceived as a veritable hit list of Chicago's best restaurants. Rather than try to mimic the cuisine of another country and turn it into some kind of foodie amusement park, Revival is quite simply a showcase for the city's finest homegrown flavors. It's a love letter to Chicago from a couple of Chicago idols.

Now downtown workers, tourists, and residents can get a taste of what makes Chicago's neighborhoods so distinguished, with modern Mexican fare from Antique Taco, warming bowls of ramen from Furious Spoon, scoops of comfort food from Black Dog Gelato, fresh bowls of raw fish from Aloha Poké Co., herbaceous cold-pressed juices from Harvest Juicery, succulent brisket sandwiches from Smoque BBQ, and even a bakery helmed by Chicago's reigning pastry queen, HotChocolate's Mindy Segal.

125 S Clark St.
773-999-9411
www.revivalfoodhall.com

ROESER'S BAKERY

Satisfying sweet tooths for more than a century

If you're wondering what makes Roeser's Bakery feel like someplace from another era, it's because it is from another era. Like a rare gem preserved in time for more than a century, the oldest family-run bakery in the city has maintained its dutiful commitment to quality, attracting generations of cake-lovers and locals.

The vintage bake shop is now in its third generation of Roeser ownership, after John Roeser Sr. came to Chicago from Germany to begin a wholesale bakery business, followed by the current bakery in 1911. He handed the reins to his son, John Jr. in 1936, who then passed it along to his son John III decades later. It was John Jr. who assembled the bakery's famous neon sign, which still stands out boldly as a Humboldt Park icon.

Although the world around Roeser's has changed a great deal, including a shift from a mostly Scandinavian enclave and a surge in newfangled bakeries throughout Chicago, the shop still utilizes the same crowd-pleasing recipes for stollen, strudel, breads, and cream cakes that have made them so endearing since day one. More than a century in and thousands of cakes later, Roeser's has stood the test of time and solidified itself as a model of familial camaraderie, community, and colorful confections.

3216 W North Ave.
773-489-6900
www.roeserscakes.com

Over the years, Roeser's has experienced a number of milestones. It was the first bakery in Chicago to feature a freezer onsite, the first all-Formica café, and the first air-conditioned bakery, which comes in handy during those cake-meltingly humid summer days.

Top Left: For more than a century, Roeser's has been a go-to for cakes, breads, and desserts of all shapes and sizes.

Top Right: Cakes are as heartwarmingly classic as they come at Humboldt Park's most iconic bakeshop.

Bottom Left: The bakery's wholesome wares include a substantial roster of freshly baked breads.

Bottom Right: From cinnamon rolls to iced Danishes, if you crave it, Roeser's has it.

SABLE KITCHEN & BAR

A River North fixture that raises the bar on bar food and cocktails

One of the best bar-restaurant hybrids in Chicago, Sable Kitchen & Bar is a breeding ground of talent. Having catapulted both chefs and mixologists to national acclaim, Sable is basically the *American Idol* of restaurants. When it opened in 2010, it broke down barriers. It was the first major restaurant to defy the stigma of "hotel restaurant."

Housed inside the Kimpton's Hotel Palomar in River North, Sable proved that a great meal and great drinks can be found anywhere, and that hotels were deserving destinations for locals. The space is sexy, dark, and elegant, harkening to a bygone era of indulgence and glamor; it's easy to see how such a unique place could appeal to a wide audience.

Sable also put an instant spotlight on opening chef Heather Terhune, who had already earned high regard for her previous work at Atwood but was now earning rave reviews on an even bigger stage. She was making "bar food" her way, tying it seamlessly with

When it comes to putting his own stamp on Sable's food menu and continuing the restaurant's legacy, Graybeal makes it personal. "Every menu needs a story. Each dish is representative of something that's very personal to me and every ingredient builds upon the narrative of my life experiences, Sable's identity, and where we are going together," explains the chef. "Ultimately, the menu is a fusing of two identities and sharing that in an exciting way for our guests."

Left: For locals and out-of-towners alike, the Sable bar is the hot spot to hang in River North. Photo by Colin Beckett

Center: Now under the direction of chef Shane Graybeal, Sable's kitchen is as solid as ever, churning out dishes at once eclectic and inspired. Photo by Colin Beckett

Right: Even Jell-O shots get the gourmet treatment, as bartenders have been known to infuse classic cocktails into gelatin for riffs on texture. Photo by Colin Beckett

the beverage program and paving the way for the whole concept of shareable dishes and upscale snacks, both of which were relatively new notions at the time.

On the beverage side, there was Mike Ryan, an alum of nationally lauded cocktail bar The Violet Hour, who finally got his time to shine by mixing some of the most interesting cocktails in the city. Having also worked as a chef, Ryan brought a fresh perspective to the drink list, looking at mixology through a more culinary lens. Hence, he created drinks that dovetailed with the food menu and balanced flavors and textures in ways typically seen on a plate. While both Terhune and Ryan have since moved on to different roles with Kimpton, their pioneering restaurant and bar lives on as one of the most impactful places in Chicago. Now under chef Shane Graybeal and head bartender Mike Jones, guests can enjoy heirloom carrots with za'atar aïoli and corn pudding with tequila syrup alongside a jalapeño- and coconut-infused gin and tonic.

Sable's groundbreaking ripple effects can still be felt throughout the industry, having set a new bar for bar food, cocktails, and how the two interact with one another. Cheers to that.

505 N State St.
312-755-9704
www.sablechicago.com

Latte art reaches new heights at this Japanese-inspired West Loop coffee shop

Sure, there's coffee, lattes, and doughnuts at Sawada, but it feels sacrilegious to simplify this groundbreaking cafe as mere coffee shop. The first U.S. venture for world-famous latte expert and Osaka native Hiroshi Sawada, his namesake shop in the West Loop specializes in espresso drinks so lustrous and artistic that it practically feels like an insult to drink them, lest you mar the design. His passion for lattes originated when he went to perpetually caffeinated Seattle to study business, acquainting himself with coffee culture and latte art at independent cafes.

When he returned to Japan, he practiced at home to hone his own latte skills with razor-sharp focus and a delicate hand. This led to enrolling in—and winning—acclaimed latte competitions like the Millrock Latte Championship and eventually opening his own shop in Japan's Shibuya district in 2010. For his U.S. entry, Sawada partnered with Hogsalt, and he was wise to hitch his wagon to the

Even the entrance to Sawada is unconventional. Although it's located in an elevated portion of Green Street Smoked Meats on the eastern side of the restaurant, it's accessible via a graffiti-clad door on Green Street. It may look like a warehouse door to someplace you shouldn't be going, but it'll lead you up a short flight of stairs and into one of the hippest cafe spaces in Chicago, complete with a vintage ping-pong table transformed into a table for latte-sipping and laptop-working.

Left: One of the most popular menu items, Sawada's Military Latte, a heady green tea creation infused with vanilla, espresso, and cocoa. Galdones Photography

Right: Between the pinball machine, the ping-pong-style table, and the skateboard pour-over machine, Sawada really brings the cool factor. Galdones Photography

shining-star hospitality group behind such local hits as Au Cheval, Maude's Liquor Bar, and Green Street Smoked Meats, inside of which Sawada is nestled.

Unlike anything else in Chicago, Sawada has the look and feel of an immersive cultural experience, like sipping espresso in a bustling Tokyo sidewalk cafe with just the right mix of grunge and rustic chic. The latte master has done an impressive job bringing a taste of his homeland to Chicago, albeit modified in subtle ways to make it all uniquely American at the same time. This includes pour-over coffee prepared on top of a custom Sawada skateboard (a nod to the fact that Sawada used to commute via skateboard to work), iced coffee infused with shochu, and signature drinks like the Military Latte, a Japanese matcha green tea tipple delicately swirled with vanilla, espresso, and cocoa.

Each latte is drizzled with precisely steamed milk over rich espresso so as to produce elaborate ribbon patterns and stunning color contrasts. Food-wise, there are doughnuts from sister spot Doughnut Vault, including a camouflage doughnut made with the same matcha and chocolate flavors as the Military Latte. Everything about this place, from the elaborate equipment to the ninja-like precision poured into every drink, sets it worlds apart from your average caffeine fix.

112 N Green St.
312-754-0431
www.sawadacoffee.com

This elegant West Loop standby ages like a fine wine

Right up there with other West Loop game-changers like Blackbird and avec, Sepia has had a profound impact in molding Chicago into the world-class dining city it is today. Ever since the restaurant opened in 2007, it's been at the forefront of the city's multifaceted dining scene, serving contemporary and beautiful food that never feels dated and always feels fresh. It's the key to longevity in the infamously erratic restaurant industry, and the person turning that key is executive chef Andrew Zimmerman.

With a culinary style hinged on seasonal ingredients and local products balanced with global flavors and contrasting textures, the dexterous chef is always cooking up something unique, making for one of the more dynamic and exciting menus in town. That dynamism can at least in part be chalked up to Zimmerman's creative upbringing, which began with him pursuing a career as a musician in his twenties before pivoting to restaurant work in New York City.

His passion for cooking quickly outpaced his passion for clubs, and before long he was graduating first in his class at the French Culinary Institute. Upon moving to Chicago in 2003 to become the chef at the Park Hyatt, his culinary career really began to hit full steam. Following acclaimed stints at MOD, del Toro, and NoMI, the chef helped lead Sepia into the local spotlight with owner

"I'm a product of the proverbial 'melting pot,'" Zimmerman proclaims of his culinary style. "I'm guided by the idea that first and foremost, things should be delicious and that excellent ingredients, solid technique, and respect for the process are the best way to achieve that goal."

Top Left: Sepia foie gras royale, the foie gras royale is basically a sundae of extravagance. Credit Paul Strabbing

Top Center: Andrew Zimmerman has a way with upgrading classics at Sepia, like this horseradish-spiced beef tartare on multigrain toast. Credit Sean Henderson

Top Right: Classic sweet flavors of peanut butter and chocolate get modernized with an oatmeal pavé and rum anglaise. Credit Paul Strabbing

Bottom Left: Sepia's opulent bar area provides the wow factor when guests first enter the restaurant.

Bottom Center: Miso and burrata take a simple beet salad to the next level. Credit Paul Strabbing

Bottom Right: Housed in a former print shop, Sepia features a tasteful mix of modern design and industrial history.

Emmanuel Nony. With Zimmerman's guiding hand in the kitchen and the restaurant's vintage charm—an Art Nouveau beauty housed in a former print shop built in 1890—Sepia felt like a classic from day one. Menus are always changing through the seasons, but diners can readily expect exquisite and accessible fine-dining fare, like wild rice arancini with burrata and ramp salsa verde, duck breast with port sausage, bass in pistou broth, and roasted rabbit with tea-soaked prunes. Altogether, thanks to the restaurant's adept team and its penchant for fusing history with the contemporary, Sepia's legacy as a Chicago classic is firmly in place.

123 N Jefferson St.
312-441-1920
www.sepiachicago.com

SHAW'S CRAB HOUSE

Chicago's place for seafood and celebration, with a side of jazz

One of the premier gems for seafood in Chicago, Shaw's is an old-school nautical destination that remains the captain of the pack even amidst a sea of slick newcomers. Rather than reinvent the wheel, the restaurant works to consistently deliver the freshest products available, ensuring that customers get their seafood at the peak of freshness.

When Shaw's originally opened in 1984, it was one of the earlier concepts for juggernaut restaurant group Lettuce Entertain You Enterprises, and it remains one of the company's most popular to this day. Back then, the company had the straightforward lofty ambition of operating the best seafood restaurant in Chicago, and with more than three decades under their belt, it's safe to say they've achieved their goals. What's kept the restaurant kicking for so many years is its knack for wholesome simplicity, allowing the quality of ingredients to shine free of excess. It's a philosophy picked up by Kevin Brown, Lettuce Entertain You's current CEO and president, who opened Shaw's after working at a crab shack on the East Coast. It was here, at the most frill-free of places, that Brown fostered a commitment to sourcing the highest-quality ingredients and giving

In more recent years, the Shaw's brand has expanded its footprint with another outpost in suburban Schaumburg. In 2015, they branched out to Chicago's Lincoln Park neighborhood with a spin-off concept called Oyster Bah, which adopts the same "less is more" approach to its seafood, featuring items like smoked trout dip, grilled oysters, clam chowder, and New Orleans-style BBQ shrimp.

Left: Salad brimming with avocado and seafood approaches comfort-food levels at Shaw's Crab House. Photo by Anjali Pinto

Center: Little known fact: Shaw's features some of the best sushi rolls downtown. Photo by Anjali Pinto

Right: Skyscraper-sized seafood towers come stocked with oysters, lobster, crab legs, and more. Photo by Anjali Pinto

his customers the best. He named the restaurant after his wife, Kristi Shaw, and her fisherman father, Charles Shaw. And as the crabby name suggests, shellfish is a particular strength here, exemplified by Shaw's vast selection of oysters heaped upon icy platters with cocktail sauce and mignonette. Then of course there's copious amounts of crab, which rotate seasonally to offer everything from Florida stone crabs and Alaskan king crab legs to Dungeness crabs and soft-shells. There's truly a crab for every craving at this shellfish wonderland. Other noteworthy items include lobster, shrimp, sushi, and even steaks, for those who like a little turf with their surf. For more affordable offerings and half-price bites and slurps, swing by for oyster bar specials between 4 p.m. and 6 p.m.

The restaurant also offers an all-you-can-eat brunch featuring many of its most popular items on a gargantuan spread. The hulking restaurant is split into a dining room and a more casual, boisterous oyster bar. Although servers in the main dining room are clad in formal outfits and tables are draped in white table cloths, the restaurant is comfortable and leisurely, while the oyster bar feels more like a lively haunt in the French Quarter. Dining here feels like a throwback to the '40s, thanks to the Art Deco architecture, the jazzy live music, and most importantly, the commitment to timeless quality.

21 E. Hubbard St.
312-527-2722
www.shawscrabhouse.com

SMOQUE BBQ

Casual Irving Park eatery slinging some of the most succulent barbecue in town

It pays to follow your dreams. The story of Smoque BBQ, one of the most revered barbecue restaurants in Chicago, is an inspiring tale of an IT consultant leaving the corporate world to pursue his passion for smoked meats. Owner Barry Sorkin's ultimate dream was to open a neighborhood barbecue restaurant, so after decamping from the corporate sector, he traversed the country exploring the various barbecue hot spots, sussing out knowledge from each region and bringing his meaty melting pot back to Chicago.

The result is a Chicago-centric barbecue spot in a city famously not known for its 'cue. Although he had no formal background in restaurants and his college degree was in journalism from Columbia College Chicago, Sorkin defied the odds in opening one of the most instantly successful restaurants in town, setting a new bar for how restaurateurs should operate. Quite simply, it's all about putting in the legwork, the research, and the hustle, pursuing a heartfelt passion, and exhibiting entrepreneurial drive. Sorkin's consultant past became instantly evident when he published his widely read barbecue manifesto in advance of Smoque's opening in 2006. The manifesto, which is still posted on the restaurant's website, is a thoughtful discourse on culinary philosophy, regional history, and backstory on Chicago barbecue, all of which served to cement the man's credibility and whet customers' appetites.

Smoque specializes in fourteen-hour dry-rubbed Austin-style beef brisket, available sliced or chopped in sandwiches or as platters. It's impossibly tender stuff, barely requiring anything more than a fork to cut through the slow-cooked juicy meat. Their St. Louis-style spare ribs are venerable as well, with a nice rub and a hearty punch of smoke flavor. Pulled pork, smoked chicken, and zesty Texas sausage are a few of the other items outfitting the concise menu. Smoque has a few housemade sauces they serve on the side, which are fun to mix and match, but the meats are delicious enough on their own that

Top: The esteemed barbecue joint also runs an outpost at the Loop's popular Revival Food Hall. Jennifer Catherine Photography

Bottom: Succulent chicken, cornbread, BBQ beans, and peach cobbler make for a winning combo.

After ten years of rampant success in Irving Park, Smoque BBQ expanded to the heart of the Loop with a location in Revival Food Hall. Now downtown denizens and office workers can get a convenient taste of Chicago's best brisket, pulled pork, and more.

they definitely don't merit any condiments. They also put a lot of care into their sides, which include brisket chili, barbecue beans, mac and cheese, and a few others. Considering its popularity, there's regularly a queue at this 'cue spot, even after more than a decade in business. It's a testament to Sorkin's impressive efforts and commitment to quality. The ambience is casual and service is friendly. Feel free to bring booze, as Smoque is BYO.

3800 N Pulaski Rd.
773-545-7427
www.smoquebbq.com

Between the cupcakes and the cupcake pancakes, there's a lot to love about this Lakeview cafe and market

Part grocery store, part cafe, and part birthplace of both the farm-to-table ethos and the brunch boom in Chicago, Southport Grocery & Cafe does a lot of things, and they do them all well. The always-bustling eatery, located on retail-packed Southport Avenue in West Lakeview, has been a neighborhood keystone since 2003. That's when owner Lisa Santos opened up shop, driven by the simple, honest philosophy of preparing wholesome, delicious food for every guest as if they were coming over to her house for a dinner party—the cozy, elongated space even has the feel of a well-appointed home.

Though she previously worked as a CPA for several years, she couldn't resist the urge to follow her lifelong passion to attend culinary school and open her own cafe. She was one of the first prominent proprietors in Chicago to advocate the local farm-to-table movement, filling up her kitchen and her grocery shelves with products from nearby purveyors. Customers from near and far quickly fell in love with her style, swooning over breakfast, brunch, and lunch dishes like oatmeal porridge, chicken and grits, and patty melts, not to mention the bakery items that were quickly developing a reputation all their own. In addition to farm-fresh ingredients and artisanal wares, the cupcake has played a notable role in Southport

Southport Grocery & Cafe has one of the best, most insightful restaurant blogs anywhere. It's routinely updated with recipe ideas, new menu items, gift ideas, profiles of staffers, and lots more.

Left: One surefire way to improve upon a brunch classic? Add brisket to the biscuits and gravy.

Right: The almighty vanilla cupcake is the ultimate comfort food and the star of the bakery at Lakeview's quintessential cafe.

Grocery's rise to prominence. Simple and addictive, in classic flavors like vanilla and chocolate, Santos's cupcakes are regarded as some of the best in the city, so much so that they inspired "cupcake pancakes"—sweet vanilla-scented flapjacks made from cupcake batter—on the brunch menu. It's no wonder this place is such a crowd-pleaser.

Over the years, Santos has rounded out her all-star team and her repertoire quite nicely. Her grocery shelves are lined with everything from Chicago-made syrups and barbecue sauces to locally roasted coffee, and she employs a designated preservationist, whose role it is to make pickles, apple butter, relishes, marmalades, and other preserves for the store shelves. The indelible legacy of Southport Grocery & Cafe is a true testament to Santos's will and her commitment to following her dreams, no matter how drastic a change it entailed. If she can do it, so can you.

3552 N Southport Ave.
773-665-0100
www.southportgrocery.com

Italian cuisine soars to new heights at this fine-dining destination on the Mag Mile

When it comes to paradigm-shifting restaurants in Chicago, few can hold a candle to Spiaggia and the envelope-pushing efforts of chef Tony Mantuano. For a cuisine like Italian, long stereotyped in the states as a grandmotherly medley of meatballs and saucy pasta, the notion of elevating it to the uppermost echelons of fine dining seemed like a fantasy when the restaurant opened in 1984.

And to add to the cheek, Mantuano opened his pricey, tasting menu-oriented Spiaggia at the tip-top of the Magnificent Mile, amid some of the splashiest real estate in the country. Right out of the gate, he was setting expectations extraordinarily high. But despite any reservations, the restaurant was a smash hit, shattering preconceived notions and heralding a new era for fine dining, and more importantly, Italian cuisine. Along with current a la carte and bar menus, ever-changing degustations include stunning interpretations of items like tonno vitellato, gnocchi, cioppino, and more.

The maestro behind it all, Mantuano exhibits refinement and panache with every plate he touches, earning the honor of being the only four-star Italian restaurant in Chicago and amassing fans like President Obama, who celebrated his 2008 victory with dinner at one of his favorite restaurants.

> "Our message with the food at Spiaggia is and always has been a personal view of Italian cooking, always using the best products. Our relationships with Italian artisans have never been so deep. We are able to get so many more quality, authentic products today, and we are more connected than ever to farmers."–Tony Mantuano

Top Left: Spiaggia, where the prosciutto looks prettier than a bouquet of flowers. Credit Haas and Haas Photography

Top Right: From fresh pastas to stunningly refined seafood dishes, Tony Mantuano serves up the wow factor at his fine Italian restaurant. Credit Haas and Haas Photography

Bottom Left: This isn't your grandma's pasta. Unless your grandma is a Michelin-starred chef. Credit Haas and Haas Photography

Bottom Right: Shellfish is so bracingly fresh at Spiaggia, you might think you're dining on the Amalfi Coast. Photo by Haas and Haas Photography

980 N Michigan Ave.
312-280-2750
www.spiaggiarestaurant.com

The vintage Americana soda fountain lives on at this adorable Humboldt Park shop

A heartwarming haven of baked goods and vintage Americana, Spinning J is a nostalgic dose of old-fashioned desserts in Humboldt Park. Here you'll find pie, housemade sodas, floats, cookies, and so much more, all housed in a gorgeous space that breathed new life into Midwestern soda fountains of yore. What's old is new again, not only in terms of refurbished countertops, but especially in terms of harkening to a bygone era in America.

The husband-wife couple behind Spinning J is Dinah Grossman and Parker Whiteway, who put down brick-and-mortar roots after several years operating Cheap Tart, a pie delivery company they ran out of a commissary kitchen. An old-timey soda fountain like the one they opened is the rare, unique opportunity for them to combine their strengths: Grossman helms the kitchen while Whiteway's background in chemistry lends itself well to phosphates, botanicals, soda recipes, and the like.

Their combined forces result in a refreshingly unique menu of Thai tea egg creams, root beer shakes, hibiscus key lime pie, addictive peanut butter cookies, and much more. There's also an abundance of delicious savory items, from rotating quiche flavors and sag paneer pot pie to breakfast sandwiches on fluffy house-baked English muffins and meat-free roasted beet Reubens. The couple poured their hearts and souls into every corner of the space too, repurposing the marble bar and stools that were originally employed by Sanger Drug in Milwaukee, the same soda shop Grossman's grandmother frequented growing up, and rounding it out with mismatched vintage glassware, a back bar made from recycled church pews and an old piano that doubles as the coffee station. Her grandmother's influence didn't end there either—the name Spinning J is inspired by her spinning jenny necklace.

Top Left: Decadent pies, ripe with Americana, are a star at the bakery. Like this s'mores version crowned with toasted marshmallow fluff. Photo by Clayton Hauck

Above Left: Key lime pie gets a colorful makeover with the addition of hibiscus and berries. Photo by Clayton Hauck

Above Right: An old Milwaukee pharmacy counter gets new life as the centerpiece of Spinning J. Photo by Clayton Hauck

From the old-meets-new motif to the soul-soothing comfort food, Grossman and Whiteway have brought the soda fountain into a new era.

1000 N California Ave.
872-829-2793
www.spinningj.com

SUN WAH BBQ

Hong Kong-style barbecue and feasts fit for the whole family

It's a very special thing when a family shares the same dream. For the Cheng family, that dream lives on at Sun Wah BBQ, a Chinese restaurant that's come a long way from its origins as a sliver of a storefront in New York City to become one of the most popular and thriving restaurants in Chicago's Uptown. The dream started with Eric Cheng, the founder and patriarch of Sun Wah. Specializing in Hong Kong-style barbecue, he got his start in New York's Chinatown before relocating to Chicago with his wife Lynda out of a desire to raise their family in a better environment. In 1987, Sun Wah took shape on Argyle Street in Uptown, standing out as one of the sole Chinese options in a heavily Vietnamese neighborhood nicknamed "Little Saigon." The restaurant quickly caught on, with diners and local families flocking to Sun Wah for its signature roast duck, plus baked chicken and barbecue pork. Since the restaurant was constantly getting busier, it presented an apt opportunity for the Cheng children to work at the restaurant, helping their parents and learning the ropes so that they would be able to carry on the family legacy. In 2008, Kelly Cheng became general manager, Laura

The star item on Sun Wah's expansive menu is the Beijing duck, a multi-course spread of barbecue duck designed to feed several diners. Although an off-menu item, it's a popular "secret" among Chicagoans. It starts with a platter of steamed bao buns for guests to compile into makeshift roast duck sandwiches. Next, the kitchen uses the carcass to simmer a duck soup, followed by a heaping portion of duck fried rice.

Top Left: Crispy duck is the most popular menu item at Sun Wah BBQ, drawing customers and groups from near and far.

Top Right: Shimmering with crackly-crispy skin, duck at Sun Wah is an essential order.

Bottom Left: The Beijing duck at Sun Wah is a multi-course off-menu feast.

Bottom Right: For one of the roast duck courses, guests stuff crispy morsels into pillowy bao buns for DIY sandwiches.

Cheng started cooking in the kitchen, and Michael Cheng headed up Sun Wah's signature barbecue offerings. They've since moved the restaurant around the corner to Broadway and expanded in size exponentially. They've come a long way since New York, and the Cheng saga proves the power of the family dream.

5039 N Broadway St.
773-769-1254
www.sunwahbbq.com

SUPERDAWG

The classic Chicago-style hot dog tradition gets a crinkle-cut twist

In a city rich with hot dog lore, Superdawg reigns supreme. Since 1948, the vintage drive-in restaurant on Chicago's far northwest side has been a tradition for families, most especially the Berman family who's been running the eatery since day one. In a way, Superdawg has always been a restaurant rooted in romance, a love story personified by the male and female hot dog characters standing side by side on the Superdawg roof to this day.

It's the story of how Maurie met Florence (aka Flaurie) and how the young couple wanted to open a business together that jibed with their schedules. With Maurie fresh off soldier duty in World War II, studying at Northwestern to become a CPA, and Flaurie teaching in the Chicago Public Schools, the pair decided to open a casual summertime hot dog stand that would work with their school commitments.

And so they did, opening their unique drive-in-style restaurant bedecked with giant hot dog characters and their own version of the Chicago-style hot dog that was unlike anything else in town. Inspired by comic books of the era, they coined the term Superdawg. The hot dogs here have a nice snap to them and a bit of pleasant spice, each one dressed with pickled green tomato, onions, sport peppers, mustard, and a pickle and served with crinkle-cut fries. By the time Maurie completed his CPA exam, the duo opted to focus full time on their successful venture and keep it open year round.

You can thank Superdawg for that hot dog emoji on your smartphone. When Apple finally added the food symbol to its operating system in 2015, it was thanks in part to companies like Superdawg pushing for it for years.

Top Left: The love story behind Superdawg all started with Maurie and Flaurie.

Above Left: Superdawg has been a family destination since 1948, when the Bermans christened their iconic hot dog drive-in on the far northwest side of Chicago.

Above Right: The Superdawg family expanded to the suburbs with an outpost in Wheeling.

They installed electronic speaker systems that enabled carhops to take orders remotely and deliver food directly to parked cars. Over the decades, not much has changed at this iconic destination. They've added a few new menu items here and there, like burgers and chicken sandwiches, along with a spin-off location in suburban Wheeling, but Superdawg remains a slice of 1940s Americana and a diamond in the hot dog rough. Maurie passed away in 2015, but his legacy lives on, and the love story that inspired Superdawg continues through the love his loyal customers have for his legacy.

6363 N Milwaukee Ave.
773-763-0660
www.superdawg.com

SWEET MANDY B'S

If an adorable bake sale evolved into a bakery, this would be it.

In a way, appeasing a sweet tooth with cupcakes is an important form of social work. Which would explain the natural segue for Sweet Mandy B's owner Cindy Levine, who pivoted from a career in social work to desserts when she opened her Lincoln Park bakery in 2002.

The avid home baker saw a void in Chicago for old-fashioned bakeries, the kind that transcend trends and satisfy comfort food cravings that appeal to all ages and walks of life. Named after her kids, Mandy and Brian, Sweet Mandy B's is redolent with aromas and visions of vintage Americana, where pastry cases brim with buttercream cakes, frosted cookies, fudgy brownies, chocolate pudding parfaits, and so much more. To this day, cupcakes are the enduring crown jewel at the sunny bakery, frequently cited as among the best in Chicago.

True to Levine's longtime vision, these aren't gourmet cupcakes that attempt to reinvent the wheel with wonky flavors. Rather, it's the humble simplicity that makes them so endearing and timeless, wherein moist cakes are crowned with heaping mounds of colorful, buttery frosting. They come in a variety of flavors, but the classic vanilla and chocolate cupcakes serve to prove that well-honed nostalgia, free of any bells and whistles, goes a long way. Sweet Mandy B's is open for breakfast through late night, making it a bit of an anomaly in the bakery world, offering muffins, scones, and cinnamon rolls in the morning before gradually filling the cases with frosted goodies and desserts as the day progresses.

A good rule of thumb here is the more colorful the icing, the better. Be it a chewy cookie, a gigantic Rice Krispies treat, a slice of layer cake, or a cupcake, the confections are not only beautiful, but exceptionally sweet and soul-soothing. All these years later and just as popular as ever, Levine's Sweet Mandy B's proves there will always be a desire for old-fashioned confections.

Top Left:Nostalgia for Americana is the name of the game at Sweet Mandy B's, where the colorful shelves are stocked with the likes of Rice Krispies treats, cookie sandwiches, puddings, and much more. Credit Sherrie Tan

Above Left: Cookies at this sunny Lincoln Park bakeshop are every kid's dream come true. Same for every kid at heart. Credit Sherrie Tan

Above Right: Pop tarts have got nothing on these hand pies. Credit Sherrie Tan

1208 W Webster Ave.
773-244-1174
www.sweetmandybs.com

Chicago's original cupcake bakery is still one of the best

People are always clamoring for the next food craze. From doughnuts to bacon, ramen to soft-serve ice cream, the hype machine is constantly on the lookout for the "next big thing" in the food industry. One of the original food crazes, the humble cupcake has really been a game-changer in regard to how consumers view their food and seek it out.

There's also a lot to be said for the fact that cupcakes have transcended their trend status to become one of the most enduring snacks in American comfort food lore. Unlike rainbow bagels or Cronuts that try to push the envelope to dazzle Instagram-happy diners, a quality cupcake will always have its place. This might explain the steady popularity of Chicago's original cupcake-exclusive bakery, Swirlz. Still just as adored and popular as the day it opened in 2006, the bakery has a simple recipe for success.

Owners/business partners Pam Rose and Brandon Mayberry start with a base of rich buttermilk cake and whipped Italian buttercream. From there, they use it as a blank canvas for any number of classic

Swirlz has been a real pioneer in regard to gluten-free pastries. In addition to distributing gluten-free cupcakes to Midwestern Whole Foods markets, the Lincoln Park shop always has unique gluten-free flavors on hand, like banana Nutella. The bakery uses organic rice flour, the same type of flour used in Japanese desserts to make mochi, specially sourced from a dedicated gluten-free facility in California that steel cuts their flour.

Left: Mini cupcakes are as adorable as they are delicious, bursting with rich flavors like chocolate and pistachio.

Right: Chicago's first dedicated cupcake shop is still among the best, baking up desserts as beautiful as handheld works of art.

and contemporary creations that have dazzled Chicagoans for years. Open for more than a decade, long after Carrie Bradshaw set the trendsetters abuzz with her cupcake purchase, Swirlz is proof that a quality product goes a long way. Over the years, Swirlz has produced upwards of 1,500 cupcake flavors, many drawing inspiration from across the globe and all containing high-quality ingredients like European-style butter from Grasslands Farm in Wisconsin, or farm-fresh berries delivered from a CSA.

In addition to classic staples like red velvet and bittersweet chocolate, look for novel flavors like churro, a vanilla cake filled with cinnamon pastry cream and topped with vanilla buttercream and a mini churro. Or the indulgent caramel brownie batter cupcake featuring a chocolate cake, brownie batter filling, chocolate ganache, brownie batter buttercream, caramel drizzle, and a dainty brownie garnish. When it's all said and done, cupcakes are as classically American as a Chicago-style hot dog. With places like Swirlz pouring attention to detail into each and every layer and element, it's easy to see why Chicago's original cupcake shop is much more than a trendy blip on the radar.

705 W Belden Ave.
773-404-2253
www.swirlzcupcakesshop.com

Classic German cuisine, classic Loop location

When it comes to family-run dining temples not only in Chicago, but in the United States at large, The Berghoff is king. It's the classic heartwarming story of a young immigrant looking to make his mark and hit it big in America. And it all started with beer. In 1870, seventeen-year-old Herman Joseph Berghoff had newly arrived in Brooklyn from Dortmund, Germany. Over the years, he moved further west, eventually establishing a brewery in Fort Wayne, Indiana. It's his Dortmunder-style beer that inspired Berghoff to open a casual eatery in Chicago as a means of bringing his product to the masses.

Dating back to 1898, The Berghoff is one of the oldest restaurants in the city, now under fourth-generation ownership. When it first emerged, Berghoff ran his business as a men's saloon serving nothing but beer from his Indiana brewery and corned beef sandwiches. Although Prohibition almost did him in, Berghoff emerged from the period stronger than ever, with a full-fledged restaurant and the first liquor license granted in Chicago after alcoholic beverages became legal again.

While the historic look and feel of the restaurant remain intact, today it features an expansive menu of classic and modern German fare. Customers from near and far visit the institution for doughy Bavarian pretzels, tangy sauerkraut-dressed knockwurst, and wiener schnitzel with German fried potatoes.

Beer is still a big deal at The Berghoff. Although brewing has moved from Fort Wayne to Wisconsin and ownership has changed, new brewers strive to keep The Berghoff tradition alive with recipes for beers like the Dortmunder Lager and the Straight Up Hefeweizen.

Top Left: Apple strudel is a fine finale at The Berghoff, made with Granny Smith apples, pecans, and golden raisins in a flaky, buttery crust.

Top Right: Seemingly preserved in time, there's something so special and comforting about one of the Loop's most iconic destinations. Photo by JT Andexler

Bottom Left: It doesn't get more quintessentially German than beer and jumbo pretzels at The Berghoff.

Bottom Right: Customers still come from near and far for a taste of Chicago's most famed schnitzel, knockwurst, and sauerbraten.

17 W Adams St.
312-427-3170
www.theberghoff.com

At the forefront of the snout-to-tail tradition since 2008

While other regional American cuisines have their own distinctions, for instance: Southern food, coastal Californian fare, and New England seafood, the Midwest has long been overlooked as a region with its own culinary voice. Thanks to pioneers like The Bristol though, that's all changing. The Bucktown restaurant was a vehement champion of the nose-to-tail movement long before that term became a cliché, and it has remained at the cutting edge of seasonally inspired, locally sourced Midwestern fare thanks to executive chef and Illinois native Chris Pandel.

Despite attending culinary school at Johnson & Wales University and working at New York City's Cafe Boulud, the Midwesterner couldn't resist the urge to come home. From his first job cooking at a local restaurant in his hometown of Riverside to time spent at fine-dining institution Tru, the chef was well versed in the multifaceted rites of Midwestern cooking. Opened in 2008 at the onset of the whole-animal dining craze, The Bristol features a diverse, exciting, and daring menu, abundant with atypical cuts of meat, equally bold vegetable dishes, eclectic flavors, and a comfortable atmosphere.

The bulk of the menu rotates on a near-daily basis, augmented with a few standby favorites, like salty monkey bread with dill butter and the egg yolk raviolo washed with brown butter. The rigorously local menu reads like an homage to the region, featuring everything from smoked Lake Superior whitefish and roasted corn agnolotti to heirloom tomatoes and pork shoulder.

The chef has such a particular knack for pasta that he's also rolling it at The Bristol's sister restaurant, Balena. The Bristol has the feel of a bustling urban cottage, what with its polished wood surfaces, chalkboard wall emblazoned with daily specials, and the generally cozy ambience. It's a fun setting in which to rub elbows with strangers and tuck into some of the most adventurously seasonal food in the Midwest.

Above Left: Every table in the cozy and snug restaurant lends itself to the action-packed environment that is The Bristol.

Top Right: Drink too much last night? Never fear, because The Bristol's hangover breakfast (noodles, pork broth, charred scallions) is just the antidote you need.

Above Right: Buttery Basque cake is a staple dessert, regularly outfitted with seasonal fruits and accompaniments. Save room.

2152 N Damen Ave.
773-862-5555
www.thebristolchicago.com

THE BUTCHER & LARDER

The friendly neighborhood butcher shop every neighborhood wants

Pulling the plug on a successful neighborhood restaurant at the height of its acclaim seems an audacious move. But for the husband-wife duo behind Bucktown's bygone Mado, the segue from full-service restaurant to butcher shop couldn't have been more natural. Opened by Rob and Allie Levitt, who met while attending the Culinary Institute of America in New York, the shop is the culmination of their dream to focus on the butchering they loved doing so much at their former restaurant, all with the overarching goal of better connecting people to their food and ultimately creating a more harmonious relationship between diners, chefs, butchers, farmers, and every facet of the food chain in between.

This was especially true for Rob, the butcher, who was increasingly developing local renown for his meat dishes and off-cuts anyway, so the leap to full-time butchery was a seamless transition. It's something he fell in love with when he first read *Cooking By Hand* and developed an interest in sausage-making in particular.

Since moving out of their original space in Noble Square and into Local Foods, Levitt is thrilled with a lot of the improvements that came with the upgrade. "I love my curing room and the ability to get more animals from lots of different farms," he says. "We have a pretty amazing setup to cut, cook, cure, and sell, and it's really inspiring to see how my staff, especially those who have been with me for a long time, have adapted into the new space and evolved their roles."

Left: The curing room at The Butcher & Larder, where all the meat magic happens.

Right: The Butcher & Larder crew is like the A-team of meat.

The Butcher & Larder is a mecca for anyone seeking out the best cuts of meat in Chicago, be it commonplace items like pork ribs and chicken drumsticks or something a little more outré, like beef neck bones or värmlandskorv sausage. All of Levitt's sources are local farms, which is fitting considering the shop is housed inside an artisanal market called Local Foods. It's a practice he's championed since his days at Mado, when the couple established relationships with nearby farmers, and it's something he strives to showcase even further via butchery, familiarizing people with unfamiliar products and showing that when animals are raised responsibly by farmers who care, the possibilities are endless.

While the menu at The Butcher & Larder focuses on take-home products, the shop also provides meats to adjoining Stock Cafe, where shoppers can sit down for lunch and feast on the likes of beef fat potatoes, sloppy joe pasties, and roast beef sandwiches with horseradish cream. Another cool aspect of shopping here is the built-in "theater" aspect to it all. Butchery is always happening right behind the counter, in plain view, so if you like meat and brisk knifework, it's prime entertainment. And between Levitt and his adept team of top-tier butchers, they're all more than happy to chat with customers about what they're doing and what kinds of meats and cuts are ideal for various uses. They even offer recurring butchering classes and demos onsite at Local Foods.

1427 W Willow St.
312-432-6575
www.localfoods.com/butcher

THE CHICAGO DINER

All-American comfort food gets a meat-free makeover

"**M**eat Free Since '83" is the slogan at this funky, longstanding vegetarian diner in Chicago's Boystown neighborhood. Apparently, the formula works because not much has changed in the thirty-plus years it's been in business, save for the addition of a second location in Logan Square, a couple of cookbooks, and going wholesale with slices of vegan cake at select Whole Foods in the Midwest.

Like a good miso paste, The Chicago Diner only gets better with age. But back in the early '80s, the notion of an entirely meat-free restaurant was an audacious one, and pretty much everyone assumed Mickey Hornick and Jo Kaucher's idea was crazy. Their crafty response was to create an all-American diner filled with hulking platters of comfort food so decadent and indulgent that no one would notice that their corned beef was actually corned "beef" made with strips of seitan. From poutine with vegan cheese and gravy to Cajun black bean burgers, from nachos with seitan chorizo to vegan chocolate chip cookie dough milkshakes, The Chicago Diner has done more for vegan and vegetarian food in Chicago than any other restaurant.

For the longtime owners, their meeting (and the idea for The Chicago Diner) was as fortuitous and surprising as their diner's rampant success. Hornick left his job at the Chicago Board of Options to take a dishwashing gig at the now-defunct Breadshop Kitchen, a place he had been frequenting as he delved further into vegetarianism for health reasons. This is where he met Kaucher, the chef helming the restaurant's bread baking. When that restaurant closed and Kaucher opted to move to California, Hornick promised her they'd meet again and open a restaurant together.

Top: There's more to this Cuban sandwich than meets the eye. Grilled marinated seitan instead of ham, for instance.

Center: As soul soothing as the beefiest meatloaf, this one contains a blend of mushrooms and lentils with white truffle-mushroom sauce.

Bottom: The Chicago Diner's milkshakes, in flavors like mint chocolate chip and peanut butter cookie dough, have a cult following. And rightfully so.

The main difference between the Boystown original and the Logan Square expansion, which opened in 2012, is the bar program. The Logan Square outpost features an expansive liquor, beer, wine, and cocktail menu, with everything from whiskey sours and hard ciders to mezcal and rosé.

Turns out, that fortuitous meeting happened in '83, and despite everyone's doubts, the now-married Hornick and Kaucher signaled a successful new era for vegetarian food in Chicago, proving that comfort food need not include meat to be deeply delicious.

Boystown:
3411 N Halsted St.
773-935-6696

Logan Square:
2333 N Milwaukee Ave.
773-252-3211

www.veggiediner.com

Pork, oysters, and beer barely scratch the surface of what this Fulton Market mainstay can do

The most ambitious concept in One Off Hospitality Group's impressive canon of restaurants, The Publican boldly flies in the face of the elegant entries that came before it. While One Off's original restaurant, Blackbird, traffics in meticulous plating and twee ingredients like smoked cauliflower and cajeta caramel, The Publican is almost brash in its riotous contrast; it takes the concept of gluttony and elevates it to an art form.

More than a decade after chef-partner Paul Kahan ascended to culinary stardom with Blackbird, he and partners Donnie Madia, Eduard Seitan, and Terry Alexander christened their pork-centric ode to European beer halls. Along with Kahan, executive chef Cosmo Goss and chef de cuisine Jacob Saben form the A-team driving the kitchen and cementing its rightful reputation as a palace of pork, oysters, and beer. For Kahan, the impetus to open a pork-centric restaurant was a natural one, considering his dad owned a

The Publican arm of One Off Hospitality Group has been so wildly successful that it's sprouted several spin-off concepts all its own. Right across the street from the original is Publican Quality Meats, a casual butcher shop, market, and cafe slinging killer sandwiches like braised pork belly gyros. The Publican Tavern also landed at O'Hare International Airport's Terminal 3, and Publican Anker opened in Wicker Park in 2016. The latter features a more casual, bar-forward version of the original, with inventive snacks like kippered mackerel, pork collar, and chimichurri-splashed apple salad.

Left: Platters of roast chicken heaped over french fries are a real crowd-pleaser. Photo by Aysegul D. Sanford

Right: The massive dining room fills to the brim with diners clamoring over shared plates of pork, oysters, and so much more. Photo by Joni Kat Anderson

delicatessen and pork is perhaps the ingredient he's got the most experience with and best reputation for.

While dishes here are still by all means composed and gorgeous, it's the rustic, indulgent approach that sets the restaurant apart so boldly from its predecessor. Almost everything is hearty and unabashedly rich, from the crowd-pleasing roast chicken served dripping atop a platter of french fries to emboldened vegetable dishes like barbecued carrots and fried broccoli with labneh cheese and spiced honey. Then of course there's the swine. The kitchen regularly receives whole pigs from local farms to butcher in-house and use in all sorts of applications, like pork belly with grits, country ribs, pork pie, and even pig brains with charred herb salsa and pomegranate.

Dining here is not for the faint of heart, nor those on a diet. The menu itself is massive, and offerings change constantly (many items daily), which means there are always new things to try each time you visit. Meshing with the European beer hall motif, The Publican features an extensive beer list curated by Adam Vavrick that spans multiple styles and origins, including some prized rare Belgian brews. Communal tables stretch the length of the cavernous room, with soaring ceilings, several smaller tables, and some enclosed booths that resemble animal pens along the wall, complete with enormous pig paintings that look like something out of *Animal Farm*. The whole experience is palpably fun, loud, and delicious, proving that when done right, excess can be a great thing.

837 W Fulton Market
312-733-9555
www.thepublicanrestaurant.com/#pork-beer-oysters

THE PURPLE PIG

Shareable Mediterranean plates that live up to their Magnificent Mile address

Nestled right off Michigan Avenue, The Purple Pig is a haven for stellar Mediterranean small plates and wines on the Magnificent Mile. Unlike most of the touristy spots choking the downtown shopping district, the restaurant is a chef-driven bastion equally befitting locals and tourists. People routinely line up for food from Jimmy Bannos Jr., a fourth-generation restaurateur and the son of pioneering chef Jimmy Bannos. In Chicago's restaurant community, the Bannos family is royalty, making Bannos Jr. the crown prince and one of the promising young talents in the city.

After years of mentorship from his father, bussing tables and working in the kitchen at his legendary Heaven on Seven, the younger Bannos finally gets his own spotlight in which to shine, and shine he does with his first-rate take on Mediterranean cuisine. Although he grew up in his dad's Cajun restaurant, Bannos Jr.'s passion for Mediterranean fare stems from his Greek heritage and his time spent traveling through Italy and working in some of New York City's finest Italian restaurants.

As the name hints, The Purple Pig has a reputation for meaty dishes that span all parts of the animal. Pork jowl, bone marrow, pig tail, and tripe are all recurring players on the menu in various forms. With a menu that often looks the length of a phone book, the chef makes sure to devote a good portion of it to cheeses and vegetable dishes too. Throughout the seasons, he pays homage to produce with dishes like heirloom tomatoes with couscous, salt-roasted beets with whipped goat cheese, and bobota, which is essentially a Greek riff on cornbread with feta, mizithra cheese, and honey. Charcuterie platters are great, but be sure to save an appetite for items you can't find elsewhere in the city, like the pork blade steak with 'nduja and honey, the pork belly rillons with honey-mead glaze, and the JLT, a twist on a BLT with pork jowl, frisée lettuce, tomato, and fried duck egg.

The bar has a nice selection of Italian wines, including an encyclopedic by-the-glass list and some Italian beers. The only

Top Left: The shareable and snackable menu is divvied up into categories like "fried items," "smears," and "antipasti." Photo by Lisa Predko

Top Right: Larger "a la plancha" plates are great dishes to "pig" out with, like morcilla sausage, pork blade steaks, and pork belly rillons with honey-mead glaze. Photo by Lisa Predko

Bottom Left: From pomegranate-flecked quail to Greek-style chicken and turkey leg confit, The Purple Pig could easily go by the name The Purple Poultry. Photo by Lisa Predko

Bottom Right: Crusty, warm bread is at its best when smeared with the likes of Greek taramasalata, eggplant caponata, and salt-cured Greek yogurt. Photo by Lisa Predko

downside of it all? As its growing popularity and its small space clash, it can result in a strenuous wait. They don't take reservations, and customers often have to wait outside. Fingers crossed the weather cooperates.

500 N Michigan Ave.
312-464-1744
www.thepurplepigchicago.com

Where the elaborate tasting-menu dishes are as beautiful as the artwork on the walls

In terms of Chicago fine dining, Tru is legend. When the Streeterville restaurant burst onto the Chicago dining scene over a decade ago, it was run by the highly acclaimed duo Rick Tramonto and Gale Gand. At the time the couple was married, with Rick leading the charge on savory plates and Gale masterminding the dessert program. While both were well regarded in their own right, it was Tru that catapulted them to culinary fame, and though they've both long since moved on, the restaurant's reputation has remained stronger than ever.

Today, Tru proves its staying power and its penchant for evolution, thanks to current chef/partner Anthony Martin, who is operating the restaurant at its highest level ever with his contemporary French fare. For the chef, Tru represents the culmination of a lifetime of passion for both food and art. As a kid, some of his fondest memories included helping his grandmother and mother bake during the holidays, all while honing his interests in painting. He initially enrolled in art school, but decamped to pursue cooking instead by attending the Pennsylvania Culinary School. His joint interests really came to a head in 2008 when he moved to Chicago to take the helm at Tru, a restaurant that doubles as an art gallery and where the food is so artfully presented that it feels like sacrilege to eat it.

Truly one of the most underrated restaurants in Chicago, Tru brings the food, the wine, the space, and the service together to form one of the most memorable dining experiences anywhere. The elegant dining room is a showcase for Tru's vast art collection, expertly exhibited by the restaurant's white walls and dark flooring. Naturally, the food is just as artful, served as part of seven- or thirteen-course tasting menus that rotate seasonally. Martin prepares dishes that are at once visually stunning and luscious, like beets with Granny Smith mousse, spiced

Tru has a dress code mandating jackets for men and "elegant-casual" evening attire for women.

Top Left: Sweet courses are as elaborate as black iced tea with ginger beer sorbet and a rhubarb cloud. Photo by Anjali Pinto

Top Right: Even something as simple as a petite summer salad is presented as a gorgeous masterpiece. Photo by Anjali Pinto

Bottom Left: For more than a decade, Tru has been at the forefront of Chicago's fine dining scene. Photo by Mark Ballogg

Bottom Right: Lamb loin gets dressed to the nines with young beets and black trumpet mushrooms. Photo by Anjali Pinto

venison with baked pear and cocoa jus, and quince and Champagne sorbet with Muscat consommé. A cheese cart wheels its way to your table after your final savory course, offering diners the option to cap off their meal with some rare cheeses. Another ritzy option is Tru's popular caviar service, presented on a coral sculpture with ten- or twenty-five-gram portions of about ten different caviars.

Tru's wine list is extraordinary as well, with more than eighteen hundred bottles sourced from around the world. An adept sommelier is on hand to guide guests through wine pairings. In addition to wine, there's a nice selection of cocktails and liquors. From its initial Tramonto-and-Gand era to its current reign under Martin, Tru is edible and visual proof that sometimes the classics are as cutting edge as they come.

676 N St. Clair St.
312-202-0001
www.trurestaurant.com

Between the rooftop farm and the green brewery, they take organic seriously around here

When Michael and Helen Cameron opened their homey Uncommon Ground in Wrigleyville in 1991, it was well before the notion of farm-to-table became the norm. Chicago's original organic farm-to-table restaurant, Uncommon Ground planted the seeds of change that have helped shape the way the restaurant industry operates, and they continue to do so with new innovations today.

From day one, the Camerons have let the seasons dictate what fills out their menus, utilizing ingredients fresh from local farms all year long. They took this one huge step further when they added the country's first certified organic rooftop farm (this means entirely chemical-free) above their Edgewater location, which opened in 2007. A legit urban farm, they grow vegetables and herbs on the eight-hundred-square-foot roof, in addition to harvesting honey from beehives.

They're also green in more ways than rooftop herbs; for example, they use repurposed wood for beer tap handles and both restaurants employ solar panels that provide 10 percent of energy throughout the year. They've even got designated cocktails that send net proceeds to funding agriculture internships for their farm.

In 2011, the Green Restaurant Association bestowed the two locations as the first and second greenest restaurants in the United States. Then in 2013, the Camerons launched Greenstar Brewing, the first organic brewery in the state, utilizing purely organic hops

A true-blue community tentpole in both Wrigleyville and Edgewater, Uncommon Ground is also revered for its live music, which takes place almost every night at each location. Both restaurants also serve as revolving art galleries for independent local artists.

Top Left: The rooftop at the Edgewater location is a certified organic farm that supplies both locations with produce, herbs, and honey.

Top Right: The restaurants are revered for their cocktail program, which boasts tasty martinis like this lemon-ginger tipple.

Bottom Left: Live music and local artwork are as prominent at Uncommon Ground as organic ingredients. Photo by Troy Burt Photography

Bottom Right: The kitchen ups the ante on meatloaf by wrapping it in bacon and topping it with charred onion gravy.

and ingredients from the restaurant's rooftop farm, like coriander seeds. That's all well and good, but these grand ambitions and efforts would all be moot if the food and drink weren't up to par. But the proof is in the pudding at these two neighborhood institutions. Or rather, the proof is in the goat cheese fondue with sweet potato fries, the Greenstar-braised pork shoulder tacos, the lavender- and honey-roasted chicken, and the grass-fed steak frites with bleu cheese Bordelaise.

Almost thirty years in and the Cameron mission is alive and well, constantly paving new uncommon ground and setting a wholesome new bar for an industry to aspire to.

Wrigleyville:
3800 N Clark St.
773-929-3680

Edgewater:
1401 W Devon Ave.
773-465-9801

www.uncommonground.com/home

Ramen lovers owe this chef-driven noodle shop a debt of gratitude

A tiny little noodle shop in an Avondale strip mall turned out to be one of the biggest foodie game-changers in Chicago. Apparently, that's what happens when one of the city's most acclaimed and promising chefs ditches the world of fine dining for something altogether opposite.

The chef in question is Bill Kim, a serious culinary talent who clocked time at Charlie Trotter's before moving on to cook at Le Lan, amassing considerable acclaim from critics and local diners for his French-Asian fare. But deep down, Kim had the itch to do something with more soul and passion, something where he could engage more with the public and cook something more personal, more comforting, on a soulful, visceral level. And so he hung up his figurative toque and pulled one of the most surprising moves in Chicago's restaurant history.

He opened urbanbelly with his wife Yvonne Cadiz-Kim in 2008, a move that would wind up having a domino effect not only in terms of a new career era for Kim, but in regard to Chicago's restaurant scene at large. Gone were the highfalutin composed dishes, in were

"I learned some important lessons from our decision to open urbanbelly, especially when people thought that our idea and location, at that time, were 'too out there,'" explains Kim:
1. "Trust your gut instincts and don't be afraid to take risks in life."
2. "Always listen to your wife. Yvonne has incredible instincts and is right about 99 percent of the time."

Left: Bill Kim's wildly popular West Loop restaurant expanded with a second location in Wicker Park in 2016.

Right: Urbanbelly built its reputation on noodles, from tofu-laden egg noodles to ramen with pork belly and egg. Credit Marcin Cymmer

the hearty bowls of slurpable ramen noodles, dumplings bursting with sweet potato and maple, and "phat rice," brimming with scrambled egg, chicken, pork, and braised beef. It's Asian-accented comfort food toeing the line between classic and contemporary, in an accessible, comfortable format that delivers high-quality, chef-driven food to the masses. This was well before that notion was a well-established concept in Chicago, not to mention years ahead of the ramen craze.

Customers flocked to the shoebox-sized eatery so much that they outgrew their space, entailing a move to larger digs in the West Loop. Kim also added an adjoining Asian BBQ restaurant called bellyQ, plus a second urbanbelly outpost in Wicker Park. It was also the beginning of a line of bottled sauces, including Belly Seoul Sauce, Belly Fire, and BellyBomb. And this being the O.G. ramen restaurant in Chicago, urbanbelly is also the host of Chicago's annual Ramenfest. By leaving the world of fine dining behind and following his heart, Kim has had more visible effect on the local dining landscape than just about any chef, and it's all thanks to a sincere love of noodles.

West Loop:
1400 W Randolph St.
773-583-0500

Wicker Park:
1542 N Damen Ave.
773-904-8606

www.urbanbellychicago.com

Indian and Latin cuisines have never been better together

When you look at Rohini Dey's many talents and accomplishments, it's clear that she's the Beyoncé of the restaurant world. It's not too often that you see a chef with "PhD" in her title. This multitalented restaurateur has a doctorate in management science from the University of Texas and a master's in economics from the Delhi School of Economics.

She formerly worked at Washington, D.C.'s World Bank, and she coauthored a book on infrastructure privatization. Oh, and she almost single-handedly pioneered a new era of Indian cuisine in Chicago. No big deal. When this powerhouse persona decided to exit her management consulting career, she did so for food.

Considering her background and schooling in Delhi, Indian cuisine has long held a special place in her heart, and it's something she wanted to highlight as a versatile, world-class cuisine on a par with the very best. With Vermilion, she fuses classic Indian flavors with newfangled techniques, presentations, and flavors, particularly those from Latin culture. Globe-trotting dishes include Venezuelan arepas with duck vindaloo curry, Nicaraguan tamales with chicken

"As an avid traveler, I've dined my way through over 50 countries and most of the U.S. Chicago has always had an extremely vibrant dining scene, from haute cuisine to dives, as well as rich global neighborhoods, so there's much more to it than the 'steak city' rap. It has an evolved and adventurous palate, sophisticated consumers, and critical mass, the three elements I really needed for my concept to succeed." –Rohini Dey

Left: Just when you thought crispy artichoke pakoras couldn't get any better, they arrive at your table via bicycle.

Right: One of the highlights of the Indian entree section, tandoori chicken masala arrives with spiced basmati rice and cooling raita

Throughout her career, and most visibly with Vermilion, Dey has been an adamant supporter of women in business. In addition to her female-driven culinary team at the restaurant, she helped found the James Beard Foundation Vermilion Women in Culinary Leadership Program and the MSEdG-Educate Girls Globally group.

kababs, and mango-chipotle chutney and Brazilian escondidinho de carne, a hearty plate of potato, Mumbai-style minced beef pie, naan, and chutney.

Dey is as well traveled as her menu too, constantly visiting countries like Peru, Chile, Spain, Sri Lanka, and beyond for inspiration. Through her entrepreneurial spirit and drive to advance world cuisines beyond the scope of stereotypes, Dey has helped shape Chicago's dining scene in more ways than most realize.

10 W Hubbard St.
312-527-4060
www.thevermilionrestaurant.com

VOLO RESTAURANT AND WINE BAR

Roscoe Village shows the rest of the city what the quintessential neighborhood restaurant looks like

Well before the idea of "neighborhood restaurants" permeated the collective conscious of the urban dining public, there was Volo Restaurant and Wine Bar. A quintessential Chicago classic in its own right and certainly a local gem in Roscoe Village, many don't realize that Volo paved the way as a pioneer of the neighborhood restaurant movement, something that's taken off exponentially in recent years throughout the city.

Opened in 2005 by chef/partner Stephen Dunne and managing partner Jon Young, Volo established the deceptively simple formula for that perfect neighborhood restaurant. It's the boutique storefront space on a pastoral street lined with independent businesses. It's the warm, timeless interior that invites guests to settle in and linger. It's the roster of affordable small plates, cheeses, sweets, and wines available by the half glass, glass, or mini carafe. It's the gorgeous backyard garden and the front sidewalk patio. In reality, the recipe for success isn't rocket science by any means, but it takes a deft team to pull it all off harmoniously. That's where Dunne and Young's collective talents come into the equation, each lending his own skill to help make Volo the bastion it remains today. Dunne's been working in kitchens since high school, when he clocked time in restaurants in the Detroit area.

After graduation, he moved to New Orleans to further his foray into cooking and broaden his repertoire at the Windsor Court Hotel. Then it was off to San Francisco, where he honed his skills and culinary philosophy at Postrio. He even spent time cooking in Paris at Lucas Carton before moving back to the Midwest and Chicago. Such a vast, varied resume really lends itself well to curating Volo's crowd-pleasing menu of eclectic, shareable dishes, like tuna niçoise salad,

Above Left: There's a little bit of something for everyone at Volo, from charcuterie and paprika chicken tacos to gorgeous plates of ahi tuna.

Top Right: Of the many key factors that make Volo the quintessential neighborhood restaurant, communal tables and a cozy, welcoming atmosphere are tops.

Above Right: When the weather's nice, the restaurant rolls out its intimate back patio, a great spot for toasting glasses filled with rosé.

smoked paprika chicken tacos, white wine-steamed mussels, pumpkin flatbread, and an Indian-accented bowl of eggplant and spinach saag. Meanwhile, Young boasts an impressive resume all his own, having managed restaurants for juggernaut groups like Lettuce Entertain You Enterprises and Rosebud Restaurants before embarking on his own with Roscoe Village's quirky staple, Kitsch'n, in 1998. Locals (and the Food Network) were quickly clamoring over his green eggs and ham. A few years later, he opened Volo right across the street, basically establishing himself as the affable mayor of Roscoe Village. For Dunne and Young, experiences in both big-name institutions and small neighborhood spots have prepared them well to join forces for what's become Chicago's most iconic neighborhood destination. And a place that makes anyone jealous who doesn't live in Roscoe Village.

2008 W Roscoe St.
773-348-4600
www.volorestaurant.com

Chicago's culinary demigod pays homage to Mexican street food

Chicago's lauded ambassador of Mexican cuisine, Rick Bayless, is at it again. Named for the Aztec word for "little sister," XOCO is the sister spot to the chef's beloved Frontera Grill and Topolobampo right next door. It's also one of the primary restaurants responsible for the wave of chef-driven casual restaurants that began sweeping the nation, giving quick-service cuisine a serious upgrade.

Here, the focus is on Mexican street food and the kinds of hearty snacks one would expect to find in a marketplace south of the border. Since Bayless never gives anything less than 110 percent, you can rest assured that this is street food like no other.

After years spent visiting and eating his way through Mexico's various states, falling in love with the country's regional cuisines and bringing his experiences back to Chicago in varied iterations, Bayless has cooked up his most transportive restaurant yet. Lining up at the perpetually bustling XOCO in River North, it's easy to feel like you're meandering through a colorful street market in Mexico City, where savory aromas mingle with freshly fried churros and vendors dart to and fro with aguas frescas and hot caldos.

Open all day, there's always something new to salivate over at XOCO, from wood-oven chilaquiles and chorizo-filled empanadas in the morning to those show-stopping tortas later in the day. These Mexican sandwiches are XOCO's bread and butter, cooked in the wood-burning oven to obtain a toasty crust brimming with fillings like succulent chorizo sausage, braised goat, and suckling pig. The ahogado is a favorite, a two-in-one soup-sandwich combo with a carnitas-filled torta immersed in spicy tomato-arbol chili broth. XOCO's giant soups, aka caldos, are the quintessential cold-weather comfort food, loaded up with chicken and pozole, braised short ribs, and potato-masa dumplings.

For a sweet finale, don't miss the crunchy cinnamon-sugar dusted churros and the hot chocolate. XOCO is the only place in town with a bean-to-cup chocolate program. This means cacao beans

Top Left: Don't come to XOCO without getting an order of fresh-from-the-fryer churros Photo by Frontera

Top Right: He did it again. Acclaimed chef Rick Bayless struck gold with his fast-casual ode to Mexican street food. Photo by Frontera

Bottom Left: Folks come from near and far and line up down the block for a taste of XOCO's wood-fired tortas. Photo by Frontera

Bottom Right: Essential to enduring Chicago winters, XOCO's warming and soulful caldos are more than soup, they're meals in a bowl. Photo by Frontera

arrive fresh from Tabasco, Mexico, to be roasted, husked, and ground onsite. Each chocolate drink is steamed with milk or water to order, and the result is an impossibly rich and thick dessert-in-a-cup.

It's this kind of intense commitment and rigorous quality that sets XOCO miles apart, or rather, eighteen hundred miles apart, since you're guaranteed to feel whisked away to Mexico.

449 N Clark St.
312-661-1434
www.rickbayless.com/restaurants/xoco

A little French, a little Asian, and a lot of love from its Lakeview community

Right in the heart of Boystown, at the corner of Halsted Street and Aldine Avenue, is a stretch designated as Honorary Yoshi Katsumura Way. It's a fitting tribute too, since the restaurant at the corner has been a pivotal player in Chicago's ever-evolving dining scene, and the namesake chef behind it, aptly nicknamed the "Mayor of Boystown," has left an indelible legacy. More than thirty years ago, Katsumura opened his "cafe" with his wife Nobuko, who still runs the restaurant after her husband's passing in 2015.

Like any restaurant worth its artisanal salt, Yoshi's has evolved with the times, adapting with each new era through the infamously transient restaurant industry. When the chef, an alum of some of the area's most elite fine-dining institutions like Le Bastille and Le Francais, opened the doors in 1982, he drew upon his experiences to create an upscale French-accented destination with dishes like foie gras and duck consommé. Steadily, he and his wife shifted into more casual and more eclectic, pivoting towards French-Japanese-

Katsumura's culinary legacy lives on in new ways, not only with the restaurant that Nobuko continues to run, but also through his kids. Mari Katsumura is the pastry chef at Lakeview's Entente, where she prepares stunning desserts like profiteroles with sour cherries, shiso, and sassafras. Ken Katsumura's resume, meanwhile, includes cooking at acclaimed fine-dining restaurant Grace and butchering at The Publican.

Left: One of the most iconic dishes on Yoshi's menu is the roasted Japanese kabocha pumpkin filled with tofu, mushrooms, and vegetables.

Right: Not your average brunch: chicken tatsuta-age with French toast and green tea crème anglaise.

Californian fusion and rounding out their offerings with sushi, risotto, wontons, and other options for the increasingly diverse neighborhood.

While he had started out strictly French, Yoshi's seamlessly morphed into the rare fusion restaurant that doesn't feel tacky or contrived. Rather, it's the kind of restaurant that honorably pays homage to the melting-pot culture prominent in cities like Chicago. When the Katsumuras went more casual thirteen years in, the thing they liked most about the shift was not just that it allowed them to expand their space into an adjoining building, but especially how their customer base had expanded to older diners, younger diners, and families with kids. As a family with kids of their own, both of whom would go on to carve out their own paths in the restaurant industry, it was a fitting progression. In the restaurant business, where restaurants age faster than iPhones, places like Yoshi's Cafe are a rare breed. Regular customers span generations (roughly 70 percent of diners are return customers), many of whom look on Nobuko as family and feel right at home in the dining room, tucking into duck liver mousse, steak au poivre, and the fan-favorite roasted kabocha pumpkin filled with tofu and mushrooms.

3257 N Halsted St.
773-248-6160
www.yoshiscafe.com

The Japanese izakaya experience comes to Avondale

One of the best Japanese restaurants in Chicago is the vision of one of the city's most esteemed fine-dining chefs. After fourteen years as chef de cuisine of the hallowed Charlie Trotter's, Matthias Merges decamped to follow his longtime goal of cooking Japanese food.

It all stemmed from a fascination with Tokyo's colorful culture, vibrant markets, and dynamic dining scene populated with binchotan grills and noodle dens. And that fascination started early for Merges, as travel and worldly cuisines have long served as a source of inspiration. Growing up in New Jersey, he would read travel books and fantasize about exploring the world. Some of his earliest cooking memories involved Japanese recipes out of the *Time-Life* series, and the allure stuck with him, even as he cooked his way through culinary school and up the career ranks at Chicago classics like Gabriel's, La Tour, and the mightiest of them all, Charlie Trotter's.

Then came Yusho, Merges's full-circle ode to Japanese cooking and culture. There's no sushi at this illustrious Avondale restaurant; rather, the chef chose to shine the spotlight on Japan's izakaya traditions. Essentially Japan's version of a pub, this is the kind of place where drinking and shareable snacking go hand in hand, oftentimes literally, as diners double-fist soy-glazed chicken wings and sake.

Merges's longtime love of travel has manifested itself beyond his first restaurant. After opening Yusho, he added Billy Sunday, a cocktail bar inspired by classic American taverns. This was followed by A10 in Chicago's Hyde Park neighborhood, where European cuisines of Italy and France take the plate. Merges also opened a Yusho in Las Vegas, which quite literally opens the door for travel.

Top Left: Some of the best fried chicken in Chicago can be found at Yusho, twice fried and dusted with green tea, with spicy dipping sauce on the side.

Top Right: Don't miss out on Yusho's nourishing noodles. Varieties change often, featuring items like pork jowl tonkatsu and chicken dumpling ramen.

Bottom Left: Grilled shishito peppers wrapped in Chinese lamb sausage may very well be the ultimate snack.

Bottom Center: Chef/owner Matthias Merges has a real flair for presentation, serving up Japanese food in wholly unique ways.

Bottom Right: Soft-serve ice cream is the staple dessert, featured in different seasonal flavors throughout the year.

An anchor of the open kitchen is the blazing hot binchotan grill, where skewered squid, steak, and shishito peppers get a quick blister before being adorned with the likes of bonito flakes, kimchi, pickled seaweed salad, and green tea glaze. Yusho is also popular for its noodles, which include ever-changing varieties like pork jowl tonkatsu, chicken dumpling ramen, and a spicy crab ramen.

The beverage program is just as intricate, featuring everything from boozy sodas and Japanese whiskey to beer from the Midwest and Japan. Yusho's design is a marvel too. Courtesy of Merges's wife Rachel Crowl, of fcSTUDIO, the restaurant sports a vivid, animated motif reminiscent of a lively Tokyo streetscape. From the food to the facade, everything about Yusho is a transportive experience that's sure to make guests fall in love with travel the way Merges did.

2853 N Kedzie Ave.
773-904-8558
www.yusho-chicago.com

RESTAURANTS A-Z

42 grams
4662 N Broadway St.

312 Chicago
136 N LaSalle St.

5411 Empanadas
2045 W North Ave.
2850 N Clark St.
1659 W Division St.
175 N Franklin St.
3715 N Southport Ave.

Acadia
1639 S Wabash Ave.

Al's #1 Italian Beef
1079 W Taylor St.

Ann Sather
909 W Belmont Ave.
3415 N Broadway St.
1147 W Granville Ave.

Antique Taco
1360 N Milwaukee Ave.

Au Cheval
800 W Randolph St.

Baker & Nosh
1303 W Wilson Ave.

Band of Bohemia
4710 N Ravenswood Ave.

Big Jones
5347 N Clark St.

Big Star
1531 N Damen Ave.

Birrieria Zaragoza
4854 S Pulaski Rd.

Bistro Campagne
4518 N Lincoln Ave.

Blackbird
619 W Randolph St.

Boka
1729 N. Halsted St.

Boleo
122 W Monroe St.

Calumet Fisheries
3259 E 95th St.

Cemitas Puebla
817 W Fulton Market

Cherry Circle Room
12 S Michigan Ave.

Coalfire
1321 W Grand Ave.
3707 N Southport Ave.

Doughnut Vault
401 N Franklin St.

Elizabeth
4835 N Western Ave.

Everest
440 S LaSalle St.

Fat Rice
2957 W Diversey Ave.

Floriole Cafe & Bakery
1220 W Webster Ave.

Forbidden Root Restaurant &
Brewery
1746 W Chicago Ave.

Frontera Grill
445 N Clark St.

Furious Spoon
1571 N Milwaukee Ave.

Geja's Cafe
340 W Armitage Ave.

Gene & Georgetti
500 N Franklin St.

Gibsons Bar and Steakhouse
1028 N Rush St.

Girl & the Goat
809 W Randolph St.

Green Zebra
1460 W Chicago Ave.

Heaven on Seven
111 N Wabash Ave.

Honey Butter Fried Chicken
3361 N Elston Ave.

Hoosier Mama Pie Company
1618 W Chicago Ave.

Hopleaf
5148 N Clark St.

HotChocolate
1747 N Damen Ave.

Intro
2300 N Lincoln Park W.

Ipsento
2035 N Western Ave.
1813 N Milwaukee Ave.

Italian Village
71 W Monroe St.

Joe's Seafood, Prime Steak &
Stone Crab
60 E Grand Ave.

J. P. Graziano
901 W Randolph St.

Katherine Anne Confections
2745 W Armitage Ave.

La Sirena Clandestina
945 W Fulton Market

Lawry's The Prime Rib
100 E Ontario St.

Longman & Eagle
2657 N Kedzie Ave.

Lou Mitchell's
565 W Jackson Blvd.

Lula Cafe
2537 N Kedzie Ave.

Manny's Cafeteria &
Delicatessen
1141 S Jefferson St.

mk The Restaurant
868 N Franklin St.

Moody Tongue Taproom
2136 S Peoria St.

more
1 E Delaware Pl.

NAHA
500 N Clark St.

Nana
3267 S Halsted St.

North Pond
2610 N Cannon Dr.

Oriole
661 W Walnut St.

Pequod's
2207 N Clybourn Ave.

Piccolo Sogno
464 N Halsted St.

Pleasant House Bakery
2119 S Halsted St.

R. J. Grunts
2056 N Lincoln Park W.

Revival Food Hall
125 S Clark St.

Roeser's Bakery
3216 W North Ave.

Sable Kitchen & Bar
505 N State St.

Sawada
112 N Green St.

Sepia
123 N Jefferson St.

Shaw's Crab House
21 E Hubbard St.

Smoque BBQ
3800 N Pulaski Rd.

Southport Grocery & Cafe
3552 N Southport Ave.

Spiaggia
980 N Michigan Ave.

Spinning J
1000 N California Ave.

Sun Wah BBQ
5039 N Broadway St.

Superdawg
6363 N Milwaukee Ave.

Sweet Mandy B's
1208 W Webster Ave.

Swirlz
705 W Belden Ave.

The Berghoff
17 W Adams St.

The Bristol
2152 N Damen Ave.

The Butcher & Larder
1427 W Willow St.

The Chicago Diner
3411 N Halsted St.
2333 N Milwaukee Ave.

The Publican
837 W Fulton Market

The Purple Pig
500 N Michigan Ave.

Tru
676 N St. Clair St.

Uncommon Ground
3800 N Clark St.
1401 W Devon Ave.

urbanbelly
1400 W Randolph St.
1542 N Damen Ave.

Vermilion
10 W Hubbard St.

Vol. 39
39 S LaSalle St.

Volo Restaurant and Wine Bar
2008 W Roscoe St.

XOCO
449 N Clark St.

Yoshi's Cafe
3257 N Halsted St.

Yusho
2853 N Kedzie Ave.

APPENDIX